Cambridge Elements ≡

Elements in Philosophy of Mind
edited by
Keith Frankish
The University of Sheffield

NON-PHYSICALIST
THEORIES OF
CONSCIOUSNESS

Hedda Hassel Mørch
Inland Norway University of Applied Sciences

CAMBRIDGE
UNIVERSITY PRESS

Shaftesbury Road, Cambridge CB2 8EA, United Kingdom

One Liberty Plaza, 20th Floor, New York, NY 10006, USA

477 Williamstown Road, Port Melbourne, VIC 3207, Australia

314–321, 3rd Floor, Plot 3, Splendor Forum, Jasola District Centre, New Delhi – 110025, India

103 Penang Road, #05–06/07, Visioncrest Commercial, Singapore 238467

Cambridge University Press is part of Cambridge University Press & Assessment, a department of the University of Cambridge.

We share the University's mission to contribute to society through the pursuit of education, learning and research at the highest international levels of excellence.

www.cambridge.org
Information on this title: www.cambridge.org/9781009462273

DOI: 10.1017/9781009317344

When citing this work, please include a reference to the DOI 10.1017/9781009317344

First published 2023

A catalogue record for this publication is available from the British Library

ISBN 978-1-009-46227-3 Hardback
ISBN 978-1-009-31733-7 Paperback
ISSN 2633-9080 (online)
ISSN 2633-9072 (print)

Non-physicalist Theories of Consciousness

Elements in Philosophy of Mind

DOI: 10.1017/9781009317344
First published online: December 2023

Hedda Hassel Mørch
Inland Norway University of Applied Sciences
Author for correspondence: Hedda Hassel Mørch, hedda.morch@inn.no

Abstract: Is consciousness a purely physical phenomenon? Most contemporary philosophers and theorists hold that it is, and take this to be supported by modern science. But a significant minority endorses non-physicalist theories such as dualism, idealism, and panpsychism, among other reasons, because it may seem impossible to fully explain consciousness, or capture what it is like to be in conscious states (such as seeing red or being in pain), in physical terms. This Element will introduce the main non-physicalist theories of consciousness and explain the most important arguments for them, and consider how they each respond to the scientific and other arguments in support of physicalism. This Element is also available as Open Access on Cambridge Core.

Keywords: consciousness, non-physicalism, dualism, panpsychism, Russellian monism

ISBNs: 9781009462273 (HB), 9781009317337 (PB), 9781009317344 (OC)
ISSNs: 2633-9080 (online), 2633-9072 (print)

Contents

Introduction

How does consciousness fit into the physical world? How do our subjective mental experiences – including our thoughts, sensations, and emotions – relate to the brain and to physical reality in general?

The predominant view among philosophers and other theorists today is physicalism. Physicalism holds that consciousness is a purely physical phenomenon. Some physicalist theories hold that consciousness consists merely in some particular type of brain activity or structure – for example, the feeling of love may consist in nothing more than some neural activity involving transmission of serotonin and oxytocin. Others take consciousness to consist in a kind of information processing, or a kind of "software" implemented by the physical "hardware" of the brain.

Physicalism is predominant mainly because it may seem strongly supported by modern science. Firstly, neuroscience indicates that our conscious states depend entirely on brain states, and the best explanation of this dependence may seem to be that conscious states *are* nothing more than brain states. Furthermore, there is strong evidence that the physical world is causally closed, that is, that all physical effects have a sufficient physical cause, indicating that if consciousness is to have any physical effects – such as producing behavior – it must itself be physical. And slowly and steadily, most other once mysterious phenomena – from celestial phenomena to diseases and most strikingly life itself (at least if we set aside the fact that life may involve consciousness) – have been explained in physical terms, so one might expect the same to happen for consciousness.

But physicalism also faces important objections. One objection claims that even though previous successes indicate that science *should* be able to explain consciousness in physical terms, it hasn't yet done so – and there are principled reasons to think it never will. For example, it seems that for any physical property neuroscience may identify as the basis of consciousness we will be left wondering: Why couldn't we just have this physical property without any conscious experience? Or, as Chalmers (1995) has put it, it seems neuroscience can only tell us *which* physical states or processes are correlated with conscious experience, not *why* the correlations hold. Relatedly, it seems that no matter how much we know about the brain of another creature – such as a bat who navigates by echolocation, as in a famous thought experiment by Nagel (1974), or a human being seeing a color that we ourselves have never experienced before – we can't deduce *what it's like* to be that creature. These *epistemic gaps* (i.e., gaps between our physical knowledge or concepts and our mental knowledge or concepts) suggest that consciousness can't be purely physical after all.

This has led a minority, but still a significant number, of philosophers and other theorists to reject physicalism in favor of theories such as dualism, idealism, and panpsychism.[1] These theories all take consciousness to be non-physical, but they differ in how they take consciousness to relate to the physical world, and also in how they understand the nature of the physical world in the first place. According to dualism, consciousness and the physical are equally real and fundamental, and interact with each other causally, whereas according to idealism – at least *subjective* idealism, the kind famously associated with George Berkeley – only consciousness is fundamentally real, and the physical world is a kind of illusion. Panpsychism, in contrast, takes the physical world to be real but pervaded by consciousness, which is to say that even fundamental particles may have simple forms of it – which our own complex consciousness somehow derives from. This is typically based on the idea that although the mental and the physical are different, they are also complementary, such that neither could exist without the other.

How can these theories respond to the scientific evidence and arguments in favor of physicalism? How exactly are they supported by the aforementioned epistemic gaps and other arguments, and what are their main advantages and disadvantages compared to each other? This Element will give an introduction to the main non-physicalist theories of consciousness and try to answer these and other important questions about them.

We will begin, in Section 1, by looking at consciousness as such and its most important features. We will then consider physicalism in more detail, including the main arguments for it – that non-physicalists need to respond to – and its main problems – that non-physicalism would help us avoid.

Section 2 considers dualism, including its main subtypes of interactionism, epiphenomenalism, and overdetermination dualism. Section 3 considers idealism, primarily the subjective or broadly Berkeleyan sort, as well as phenomenalism, a closely related view. Section 4 considers theories jointly known as dual-aspect monism – because they take reality to consist of one kind of stuff with two complementary aspects, the physical and the mental or protomental – or alternatively, Russellian monism, after Bertrand Russell, who defended many of its central claims. Dual-aspect monism includes the most important version of panpsychism, but also comes in non-panpsychist versions. There is also a *pure* or idealist version of the view, which differs importantly from subjective idealism, and will therefore be discussed in this rather than the previous section.

---

[1] According to a recent survey of professional philosophers (Bourget and Chalmers ms), 52 percent of respondents accept or lean towards physicalism and 32 percent accept or lean towards non-physicalism.

1 Consciousness and Physicalism

1.1 Consciousness

The term "consciousness" can be understood in different ways. For example, consciousness can be understood as the ability to think and reason, the ability to register and process information about one's environment and oneself, or a kind of general reflective awareness. These definitions are all tied to various functions or abilities distinctive of humans or some broader class of animals. Consciousness in the sense of any mere functions or abilities can be referred to as *functional* consciousness.

There is also another sense of consciousness, known as *phenomenal* consciousness. Phenomenally conscious states are characterized by the fact that there is *something that it's like* for a creature or entity to be in them, or that they are subjectively experienced or felt. Think of experiences such as seeing red, feeling pain, tasting chocolate, feeling love, or thinking a thought. These experiences may be associated with various functions or abilities, such as perception or reflection, but they also seem to have a subjective quality or feeling to them that goes beyond that. That is their phenomenal aspect.[2]

It is phenomenal consciousness that is mainly at issue in the debate between physicalism and non-physicalism – as we will see, functional consciousness gives comparably little reason to doubt whether reality is purely physical. Let us look more closely at some of the most important features of phenomenal consciousness.

The definition of consciousness in terms of there being *something that it's like* is due to Nagel (1974), and has been widely adopted in philosophy.[3] As Nagel notes, to say that consciousness is *like* something is not to say that it merely *resembles* something (if so, everything would trivially be conscious, because everything resembles something else in some way or other). The important point, according to Nagel, is rather that there is something that it's like to be in conscious states *for* the conscious entity itself. That is, consciousness is *subjective* in the sense that it's present only for its subject or from a particular point of view. Physical objects, in contrast, are *objective*, in the sense that they can be present from multiple points of view or independently of any point of view at all – for example, different people can see, feel, or otherwise perceive the same

---

[2] The term "phenomenal" relates to "phenomena" in the sense of what immediately *appear* to us, as opposed to the reality behind the appearances. Conscious states can be regarded as phenomena in this sense because they are what immediately appear to us, and that through which the rest of reality appears (i.e., via conscious perception).

[3] The phrase was used to *describe* consciousness long before Nagel, but he seems to have been the first to *define* it in those terms (Stoljar 2016).

chair from different points of view, and we usually think that the chair can exist without anyone perceiving or having a point of view on it at all.

The claim that consciousness is subjective, in this sense, is close to another common claim, namely that consciousness is *private*. To say that one's conscious states are private does not mean that nobody else can know anything about them; it rather means that nobody else can know about them *in the same direct way*. That is, my own conscious states appear directly to me, whereas the conscious states of other people we infer or perceive indirectly through their behavior, verbal reports, facial expressions, and so on.

Because of this direct access, many philosophers also hold that our own consciousness can be known with absolute *certainty*. René Descartes famously claimed that we have indubitable knowledge of our own consciousness, and thereby our own existence ("*cogito ergo sum*"). Others, including non-physicalists[4] such as Chalmers, hold that our own consciousness is known with a high degree of certainty, but without being absolutely certain (Chalmers 2019b).

The fact that we seem to have no direct access to the consciousness of others, on the other hand, gives rise to *the problem of other minds* – how do you know that others are conscious at all? In response to this problem, some may draw the conclusion of *solipsism*, the view that nobody is conscious except oneself.[5] However, it's perfectly coherent to hold that we have privileged, direct access to our own consciousness, but can also be more than reasonably sure that other people are conscious based on indirect access by way of behavioral, verbal, and other cues.

In addition to their subjectivity, conscious states are characterized by particular *qualities*, often referred to as *qualia* or phenomenal qualities. Phenomenal qualities relate, in various ways, to physical qualities in the external world. For example, the physical redness of an apple might cause you to experience phenomenal redness (and thereby perceive that the apple is red). But you could also experience phenomenal redness in a dream or hallucination, with no physically red objects around. Conversely, the physical redness of the apple does not disappear when nobody is looking at it and no experiences of phenomenal redness occur (except according to some versions of subjective idealism, discussed in Section 3). Furthermore, science has revealed that physical qualities such as colors consist in properties such as reflecting light waves within

---

[4] Among physicalists, it's more common to doubt the absolute certainty of consciousness, given the problem it poses for physicalism.

[5] More specifically, this can be referred to as *phenomenal* solipsism, whereas solipsism in general can be understood as the view that nothing exists (i.e., neither conscious nor non-conscious beings) except oneself.

a certain spectrum and absorbing others,[6] and these properties bear little resemblance to the phenomenal qualities they cause us to experience (indeed, some hold that physical properties have been revealed as not really qualitative at all, but rather purely *structural* – more on this in Section 4). Phenomenal qualities thereby seem quite distinct from physical qualities or properties.

Going back to the definition of phenomenal consciousness as there being something that it's like for the subject, we said that the *"for* the subject" part points to the subjective aspect of consciousness. But in addition, the "something that it's like" part can be understood as pointing to, not just the trivial fact that consciousness resembles something, but rather its qualitative aspect, that is, that consciousness is *qualitatively* like something.[7]

Phenomenal consciousness is also characterized by a distinctive kind of *unity* (Bayne and Chalmers 2003). At any given time, you may have multiple experiences with different phenomenal qualities: different colors, sounds, thoughts, emotions, and so on all at once. Yet, these qualities are all unified or subsumed under a single point of view. One might think this unity results from the fact that all the qualities are experienced by the same subject, where the subject is understood as an entity, thing, or container distinct from the experiences it's having. Alternatively, one might think the unity results from the qualities or individual experiences merging together to form a single total experience, thereby forming connections directly among themselves rather than via a distinct subject. This is roughly in accordance with David Hume's claim that the self is just a "bundle of perceptions" as opposed to an entity distinct from them. It can be referred to as *the deflationary view* of the subject (since it "deflates" it from a thing in its own right to a structure of experiences related in a certain way).

A further important property of consciousness is *intentionality*. Intentionality is the way thoughts, intentions, and other mental states can be *about* things or states in the world, or *directed* or *aimed* towards them. For example, my thought that "cats sleep a lot" is *about* actual cats, in a way it seems non-mental states cannot be, at least not non-derivatively. For example, the phrase "cats sleep a lot" as printed on this page is a string of physical symbols that is also about

---

[6] At least this is a common conception. Some theories of color, such as naïve realism, hold that physical colors are more like they intuitively seem than how science tends to describe them, and more closely related to phenomenal qualities (see Maund 2018 for an overview of this and other theories of color), though they would still differ, e.g., in existing even when unperceived.

[7] See, e.g., Chalmers, who explicates that "a mental state is conscious if there is something it is like to be in that mental state. To put it another way, we can say that a mental state is conscious if it has a qualitative feel – an associated quality of experience" (1996, p. 4). Here, Chalmers explicates "something that it is like"-ness in terms of qualitativeness alone, and he also leaves the "for the subject" part out of the definition (many other philosophers tend to do the same).

actual cats, but on the face of it, this is only because one or more conscious beings have decided that these symbols should represent them, and their intentionality thereby seems derivative of the intentionality of consciousness (Searle 1983). Franz Brentano famously declared intentionality "the mark of the mental," that is, its defining feature. Today, however, philosophers tend to regard phenomenality, or "what it's like"-ness, as an equally, if not more, important mark.[8]

1.2 Physicalism

Physicalism can be defined as the view that everything, including consciousness, is *identical to* or *constituted by* physical states or processes (or physical facts, events or other categories one may prefer), that is, states or processes whose properties are all physical.[9] To say that consciousness is constituted by the physical can be regarded as compatible with saying consciousness is *realized* by, *reducible* to or *grounded* in the physical, which are other ways physicalism has been defined (i.e., constitution can be regarded as encompassing these other relations). What these relations have in common is that they all imply that consciousness is somehow *nothing over and above* the physical. Note that identity can technically be regarded as a type of constitution (insofar as everything constitutes itself), and physicalism could therefore be defined even more simply in terms of constitution alone.

There are two main types of physicalism: identity theory and functionalism.[10] The identity theory takes conscious states to be constituted by specific physical states or processes (Place 1956; Smart 1959; Searle 1992). For example, the feeling of pain may be constituted by c-fibers firing,[11] seeing red by some neural

---

[8] That is, some would deny that phenomenality is a *defining* feature of the mental because there may be unconscious (and hence non-phenomenal) mental states, but it is still widely regarded as (among) its most *important* feature in the sense of, e.g., the most interesting or mysterious. One might also hold that unconscious mental states must be at least *potentially* conscious, and hence potentially phenomenal.

[9] One might narrow the definition by adding that everything in *concrete* reality is physical or physically constituted, because some philosophers hold that abstract objects such as numbers and sets really exist in an abstract sense, and physicalism can be regarded as compatible with non-physical abstract objects. Alternatively, one might just focus on physicalism about consciousness specifically, i.e., the view that consciousness (but not necessarily reality as a whole) is physical or physically constituted, which is also compatible with abstract objects (or other objects or properties unrelated to consciousness) being non-physical.

[10] For a more detailed introduction to the various types of physicalism, see Pete Mandik's Element *Physicalist Theories of Consciousness*.

[11] Note that this and most other examples in this Element of physical states that could be regarded as the basis or correlates of various conscious states should be regarded as hypothetical possible candidates rather than plausible actual candidates. C-fibers firing, in particular, actually seems like a precursor of pain rather than the correlate of pain itself, but it has nevertheless become a standard example in philosophy of a hypothetical pain correlate.

activity in the visual cortex, or the feeling of love by neural activity in some other part of the brain involving serotonin and oxytocin.

Functionalism takes conscious states to be functional states, that is, states defined merely in terms of their causes and effects (on behavior, internal states, or other functional states), that are *realized* (i.e., implemented or performed) by physical states or processes (Putnam 1967; Armstrong 1981) (as noted, realization can in turn be regarded as a form of constitution). For example, pain could be understood (very roughly) as something like "the kind of state that makes creatures aware of possible bodily damage and in turn try to avoid it." In humans, this function may be realized by, for example, c-fibers firing, but in insects (if they feel pain) it would be realized by some other organic process, whereas in conscious robots (which would be possible, according to functionalism, if robots could replicate our functions) it would be realized by some synthetic process or mechanism.

Many functionalists take the functions of consciousness to involve computational states, or dispositions to process information in the same sense computers do. Given this kind of functionalism, consciousness could be regarded as a kind of software with the brain as hardware – or rather *one* type of hardware among others. Identity theorists, in contrast, would identify consciousness with the hardware of the brain itself.[12]

Physicalists thereby differ in exactly what kind of physical state or process they take consciousness to be. But what does it mean for a state or process (or property, fact, or similar) to be physical in the first place? On one definition, to be physical is the same as to be *material*, or made of matter. But according to physics, many things are not material in the sense of having, for example, mass, solidity or extension, which are properties traditionally regarded as essential to matter.[13] For example, many particles have no mass, and can be understood as extensionless points.

Another definition therefore leaves the specific nature of the physical up to the science of physics, by defining physical properties simply as whatever properties are described by physics (Smart 1978; Braddon-Mitchell and Jackson 1996; Melnyk 2003). Since physics describes properties beyond mass and extension, things can be physical without having these properties, but rather in virtue of having other properties described by physics such as energy or being associated with a field.

---

[12] Or alternatively, with functions that are realized by a specific type of hardware, as identity theorists may take consciousness to be partially constituted by functions and partially constituted by specific realizers.

[13] For this reason, the term "materialism" has largely been replaced by "physicalism," though the former is still in use.

However, *current* physics is certainly incomplete and even false in some respects (we know this, among other reasons, because quantum mechanics and the relativity theory, the two major components of current physics, are mutually inconsistent). Therefore, it seems physical properties should be understood as the kinds of properties described by future, *completed* or *ideal* physics.

But this leads to another objection, namely that we have no idea what completed physics will look like. If we don't put some further restrictions on what it could look like, then anything could in principle count as physical. For example, what if completed physics ended up positing immortal souls, that are completely distinct from brain processes, as equally fundamental as quarks and electrons? Or if consciousness in any form turned out to be fundamental? To say that something is *fundamental* is to say that it's not constituted by anything else, but is rather a basic building block of reality. It seems that consciousness being fundamental should be regarded as incompatible with physicalism – rather, it's typically regarded as a defining feature of most (though not all) kinds of non-physicalism.

This problem – that physicalism is either false, if the physical is defined in terms of current physics, or trivial or empty (by ruling nothing out, including theories we would typically regard as non-physicalist), if it's defined in terms of future, completed physics – was first raised by Hempel (1969) and is hence known as Hempel's dilemma.

To resolve the dilemma, one could add to the definition that physical properties should be described by a completed physics that is also *continuous* with current physics. Since fundamental immortal souls, and fundamental consciousness in general, are sharply discontinuous with anything posited by current physics, they would not count as physical (thus, if completed physics included this, physicalism would be refuted).

Another option (defended by, e.g., Montero and Papineau 2005; Stoljar 2010) is to define the physical negatively, or in terms of what it is not. Specifically, it has been proposed that physical properties should be defined as properties that are not fundamentally mental or consciousness-involving. Neither should they be fundamentally divine or have other features that clearly seem non-physical, such as protomental features (as posited by some forms of dual-aspect monism, discussed in Section 4). This negative definition can also be combined with the physics-based definition, by saying that the physical should *both* be described by completed physics *and* fulfill the negative criterion (Chalmers 1996; Wilson 2006).

In what follows, we will understand the terms "physical" and "physicalism" roughly in terms of a combination of these definitions. Physicalism should thus be understood as the view that the fundamental constituents of reality can be fully described by completed physics of a sort roughly continuous with current physics and that does not take consciousness, protoconsciousness and similar as fundamental.[14] Correspondingly, non-physicalism about consciousness will be understood as the view that the fundamental constituents of reality are *not* fully describable by completed, continuous physics because consciousness is either fundamental or constituted by something discontinuous with current physics and/or ruled out by the negative criterion, such as fundamental protoconsciousness.

1.3 Arguments for Physicalism

Until fairly recently (the 1950s–60s are typically regarded as the turning point, though the 1860s have also been identified as important [Papineau 2001, p. 5; Stoljar 2010, pp. 1–2]), non-physicalism was the predominant view of consciousness – most philosophers seemed to be idealists or dualists.

In large part, this was because consciousness just seems different from any physical properties. As we have already said, phenomenal consciousness is subjective whereas the physical is objective, and consciousness is characterized by phenomenal qualities which seem quite different from physical qualities or properties. The functions and abilities associated with consciousness are also very different from those of non-conscious beings – they involve purposeful behavior, intelligence, language, and so on – and it used to be hard to see how these functions could be performed by mere physical matter.[15]

Physicalism started to dominate only in view of a number of developments of modern science, which form the basis for three important arguments: the argument from mind–brain correlations, the argument from physical causal closure, and the argument from previous explanatory successes of science.

1.3.1 The Argument from Mind–Brain Correlations

Science has gradually revealed a strong dependence between the mind and the brain. A striking early indication of this was the case of Phineas Gage (1823–60), a railroad worker who suffered an accident in which a metal rod was pierced through his brain (see Figure 1), yet he miraculously survived. But the accident led to a radical change in his personality: before, he was described as balanced

---

[14] The physical and physicalism may also be defined in a broader sense (Stoljar 2001; Strawson 2006b; Chalmers 2013), according to which physical properties may also include properties beyond the reach of physics (such as the intrinsic properties discussed in Section 4). But this definition would include views such as dual-aspect monism and property dualism, that are typically regarded as non-physicalist and don't correspond to how the term is most typically used, and it will therefore not be used here.

[15] See, e.g., Descartes' *Discourse on Method* (Part V), where he claims that no physical mechanism could explain language and intelligent behavior.

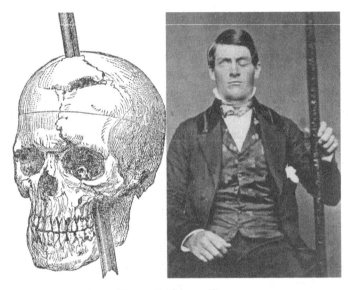

Figure 1 Phineas Gage

(**Source:** Wikimedia Commons)

and well-liked, but afterwards as "gross, profane, coarse, and vulgar" and "no longer Gage" (Macmillan 2000). If someone's personality can fundamentally change based on brain injury alone, it indicates a strong dependence of the mind on the brain.

Since then, neuroscience has offered more and more evidence for such dependence. We have discovered how consciousness can be affected by all kinds of physical events and interventions including not only severe injuries such as Gage's, but also brain tumors, syndromes (such as Alzheimer's), surgery (e.g., lobotomy or callosectomy), electromagnetic stimulation (from electroshock therapy to transmagnetic stimulation), and drugs (from anesthetics to LSD and antidepressants). And with the help of brain scanning techniques such as PET and fMRI (see Figure 2) we have discovered detailed correlations between specific conscious states and brain states (e.g., seeing red may correlate with specific activity in the visual cortex, anxiety with an overactive amygdala, and so on).

All this can be taken to support a type of correlation known as *supervenience* between mind and brain. If A supervenes on B, there can be no change in A without a change in B. Thus, if consciousness supervenes on the brain, there can be no change in consciousness without a corresponding brain change (there can, however, be a brain change without change in consciousness, because not everything in the brain makes a difference to consciousness).

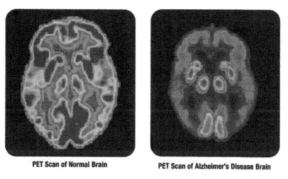

PET Scan of Normal Brain   PET Scan of Alzheimer's Disease Brain

Figure 2 Brain images obtained by PET scans

What explains this supervenience? Physicalists (e.g., Smart 1959; Hill 1991; Block and Stalnaker 1999; McLaughlin 2001; Melnyk 2003) have argued that the best explanation is that conscious states are constituted by the brain states they supervene on. The most natural alternative is a dualist explanation, according to which non-physical consciousness is connected to the brain by means of fundamental laws of nature. The physicalist explanation is simpler and more elegant than the dualist explanation in that it doesn't require positing extra laws of nature, and allows us to regard mind and brain as one thing rather than two. Other non-physicalist explanations, such as idealist and dual-aspect monist explanations, would also have to be regarded as unnecessarily complicated or otherwise implausible (though proponents of this argument tend to not explicitly focus on these alternatives).

1.3.2 The Argument from Physical Causal Closure

The argument from mind–brain correlations focuses on how the physical brain affects consciousness. The argument from physical causal closure (Kim 1989; Papineau 2001; Melnyk 2003; Montero and Papineau 2016) focuses on how consciousness affects the brain and body, or the physical world in general.

We take for granted that our conscious states have causal effects on the brain and body. If I feel pain from my arm being in an awkward position, that will cause me to move it. If I enjoy the taste of an apple, that will make me take another bite. If I have an intention to go for a walk, that will cause me to do it. And so on.

Yet, if consciousness is non-physical, it's hard to see how this is possible, in view of the *principle of physical causal closure*. According to this principle, every physical effect, i.e., event that has a cause, has a complete physical cause. That is, some physical events, such as quantum events, may be truly random and without a cause, but those physical events that *do* have a cause – and this seems to include all human behavior[16] – have a complete explanation in terms of physical causes.

Consider the case of someone moving their arm away from a painful position. This would have a complete physical explanation in terms of the nerves in their arm being stimulated by the way the arm is positioned, which causes electrical signals to be sent through their nervous system up to the brain, where it triggers the release of various neurotransmitters between neurons, culminating in a new electrical signal being sent back through the nervous system down to the arm, where the electricity causes their muscles to contract in such a way that the arm moves. We can thus explain (at least very roughly, in the case of this example) how behavior is produced without the mention of any conscious states, such as the feeling of pain or the intention to move the arm.

Furthermore, the signaling between the neurons can be regarded as implementing a kind of computation, with the neurons firing or not firing corresponding roughly to transistors in a computer turning on and off and thus representing 1's and 0's. This can physically explain (also very roughly) how our behavior can arise *intelligently*, or in a way influenced by and coherent with information received from perception, memory and so on.

As mentioned earlier, before modern science, the functions and abilities of conscious beings, such as intelligence and purposeful behavior, looked difficult to explain in physical terms, and this was one reason many regarded consciousness as non-physical. If all our functions and behaviors have a complete physical explanation after all, as the principle of physical causal closure claims, this reason to hold that consciousness is non-physical is undermined. But one might still think consciousness is non-physical for other reasons (such as it just seeming different from the physical). The *argument* from physical causal closure, however, combines the principle with two further premises in order to rule out non-physical consciousness altogether.

The principle of physical causal closure, by itself, rules out *interactionist* dualism, the view that conscious states are non-physical and cause physical effects different from those that would result from physical causes alone. But given the principle, non-physical consciousness could still be regarded as having

---

[16] A contrary view, that human behavior is rather a result of quantum randomness, will be discussed in Section 2.

no physical effects at all, as per *epiphenomenalism*. On this view, non-physical consciousness is produced or affected by physical brain states, but causes no physical effects in return. Another possibility is that our behavior has mental causes *in addition* to their sufficient physical causes. That is, our behavior might be *overdetermined* by more than one cause, both a physical brain state (that would have been sufficient to cause the behavior on its own) and non-physical conscious state (that is nevertheless present to also cause the exact same behavior).

The argument therefore adds that both epiphenomenalism and overdetermination are unacceptable, and that the only way to avoid them, if the principle of physical causal closure is correct, is to assume that conscious states are physical. If so, they could cause physical behavior, in a non-overdetermining way, in virtue of being constituted by physical brain states that we know cause behavior. Thus, physicalism offers the only plausible way of securing *mental causation*, i.e., that mental states cause physical effects, given physical causal closure.

To sum up the argument:

1. **Physical causal closure:** Every physical effect (i.e., event that has a cause) has a sufficient physical cause.
2. **Non-epiphenomenalism:** Conscious states have physical effects (i.e., behavior).
3. **Non-overdetermination:** The physical effects of conscious states (i.e., behavior) do not have more than one sufficient cause.

Therefore,

4. **Physicalism**: Conscious states are physical.

Another way of understanding the argument is as claiming that there are four possible positions one may take on mental causation, interactionism (which implies violation of physical causal closure), epiphenomenalism, overdetermination, and physicalism, among which physicalism is the most plausible option. The positions can be illustrated as in Figure 3.

Why should we believe in the premises of this argument, or that physicalism is indeed the most plausible option? Epiphenomenalism and overdetermination seem quite implausible to most people, among other things because it just seems obvious that consciousness causes behavior, and it would seem like a strange coincidence that consciousness should always cause the exact same effects as the brain states they are correlated with (these and other arguments against epiphenomenalism and overdetermination will be discussed in more detail in Section 2).

The principle of physical causal closure can be supported by scientific evidence. Many have seen it as supported by the law of conservation of energy

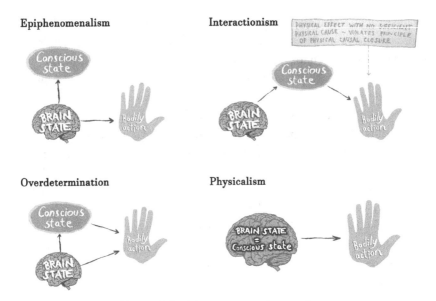

Figure 3 Positions on mental causation

(see Montero 2006, p. 384), because it may seem that if anything non-physical affects the physical world, it would add energy to it, thus violating conservation. However, one might think non-physical causes can only transfer energy to the physical that it previously received from it. If so, non-physical causes would be compatible with conservation of energy (Papineau 2001; Montero 2006). On the other hand, the scientific evidence could be interpreted as supporting not only that energy in general is conserved, but that *physical* energy is (Koksvik 2007). This is more of a threat to non-physical causes. But it's debatable whether the evidence should be interpreted in this stronger way.

A more definitive argument derives from physiology, neuroscience, and other sciences of the human body in particular (Papineau 2001). These sciences have revealed no sign of non-physical forces operating in the brain and body, which are the places influence from non-physical consciousness would be expected to show up. On the contrary, they strongly indicate that every physical event in the brain and body can be completely explained in physical terms. For example, as outlined earlier, we can explain why someone moves away from a painful position in terms of purely physical mechanisms. Of course, we don't yet have complete physical explanations of all physical behavior, because we haven't yet been able to map out every physical detail in the brain and body, so it can't be definitively ruled out that signs of non-physical influence will eventually show up. But from the fact that every physical event in the brain and body examined *so far* has seemed completely physically explicable, and our research has reached an advanced stage, we can conclude that most likely they all are.

1.3.3 The Argument from Previous Explanatory Successes

The argument from previous explanatory successes points to how most other once mysterious phenomena have one by one been explained in physical terms. For example, before the scientific revolution, stars and planets were regarded as consisting of a different type of matter than things on Earth (since celestial bodies moved in circles whereas things on Earth moved downward in straight lines), and diseases were explained in terms of evil spirits or divine punishment. And even long after the scientific revolution, life was explained in terms of non-physical, vital forces (*élan vital*). But all these phenomena were eventually explained in physical terms by means of Newtonian physics, Pasteur's germ theory,[17] and Darwin's theory of evolution combined with Francis and Crick's discovery of DNA. In addition, as also noted by the arguments for physical causal closure discussed previously, many of the major functions associated with consciousness (such as information processing and production of intelligent behavior) have already been physically explained, at least to a large extent.

According to physicalists (e.g., Smart 1959; Melnyk 2003), we can conclude from this that consciousness itself (or its phenomenal or non-functional aspects) will eventually be physically explained, too. The reason why consciousness is so late to be fully physically explained may be that the brain is just far more complex than any other known physical phenomenon.

Note that this argument is different from the argument from physiology in support of the principle of physical causal closure, according to which all physical events discovered in the brain and body so far seem to have a physical explanation, therefore we should expect all physical events (including so far unexamined or not fully explained events) to have a physical explanation. The argument from physiology concludes that all *physical events* (including those we usually take to be explained by consciousness) have a physical explanation, whereas the argument from previous explanatory successes concludes that *consciousness itself* has a physical explanation.

1.4 Arguments against Physicalism

In view of these three arguments, physicalism has become the default view within philosophy and science. The main reason why it has nevertheless not completely taken over[18] is a set of three arguments against it: the knowledge argument, the

---

[17] Diseases were also explained by the humor theory, which could be regarded as physicalistic, but unlike the germ theory this turned out false (and thus only the germ theory can be regarded as definitively supplanting the non-physical explanations).

[18] At least if speaking of physicalism about consciousness – if speaking of non-physicalism in general, arguments based on, e.g., the existence of a non-physical God or abstract objects (see footnote 9), might be at least as important.

conceivability argument and the explanatory argument. These arguments mainly concern phenomenal consciousness. In addition, there are arguments based on intentionality and unity, though they can be regarded as at least somewhat less powerful.

1.4.1 The Knowledge Argument

The knowledge argument claims that knowledge of consciousness can't be deduced from any physical knowledge; therefore, consciousness is not physical. The most discussed versions of this argument are due to Nagel (1974) and Jackson (1982).[19]

Nagel argues that if bats are phenomenally conscious (as seems plausible that they are), they would have experiences very different from ours, because they have a very different sensory system based on echolocating sonars (i.e., they generate high-pitched sounds and register how they are echoed back to them). But no matter how much we learn about the physical characteristics of the bat's sensory system, brain, and so on, we can't deduce *what it's like* to be the bat. Phenomenal facts must therefore be different from physical facts (at least, according to Nagel, on any typical understanding of the physical, corresponding roughly to the physics-based definition discussed in Section 1.2).

A possible objection to this argument is that since human brains are not configured to have sonar experiences, it's not configured to imagine them either. So, the argument only demonstrates a limit to our imagination, not a limit to what is in principle deducible. Jackson's version of the argument avoids this objection, because it appeals to a kind of experience most humans are capable of having, namely the experience of seeing red.

Jackson's version of the argument is based on a thought experiment about a brilliant scientist called Mary, who grows up in a room where everything is black and white and has therefore never seen any colors. But in the room, she has gained complete knowledge of every physical fact about colors and colors vision from black and white books. One day she is let out the room and sees a red rose for the first time. She exclaims: "Wow! So this is what it's like to see red." In other words, Mary learns a new, phenomenal fact. But since she already knew all the physical facts about red and other colors, this must be a non-physical fact.

1.4.2 The Conceivability Argument

The conceivability argument claims that it's conceivable that consciousness comes apart from the physical; therefore, it's also possible that they come apart

---

[19] Note that Jackson later recanted the argument and endorsed physicalism, but his criticism has convinced far fewer than the original argument itself.

and consciousness is not physical. The conceivability argument goes back to Descartes (*Meditations*, VI; *Discourse on Method*, IV), who argued that we can conceive of consciousness existing without the body, or any physical world at all (as the physical world could conceivably be an illusion created by an evil demon), and that we can therefore see that consciousness is distinct from the physical. This version of the argument can be referred to as *the argument from disembodiment*.

Modern versions of the conceivability argument focus on how the physical world is also conceivable without consciousness.[20] One of the most discussed versions of this kind of argument is Chalmers' *zombie argument* (1996, 2009) (see also Kirk 1974 and Kripke 1980 for important precursors). Zombies are defined as beings who are identical to us in every physical respect, including both their external behavior and their internal composition and structure – they have the exact same brain states. But they lack phenomenal consciousness – there is nothing that it's like to be them. Chalmers argues that (1) zombies are perfectly conceivable, (2) if zombies are conceivable, then they are *metaphysically possible*, and (3) if zombies are metaphysically possible then physicalism is false.

Metaphysical possibility is roughly equal to logical or conceptual possibility – that is, to not involving any contradiction in terms, as the concepts of "married bachelor" or "square circle" do – or possibility in principle.[21] It should not be confused with *nomological possibility*, which is possibility given the actual laws of nature. Clearly, conceivability does not imply nomological possibility, as we can conceive of a number of things that are not possible given the actual laws of nature, such as people levitating, faster than light travel, and so on. But conceivability may plausibly be regarded as a guide to metaphysical possibility.

More precisely, the zombie argument takes conceivability to imply metaphysical possibility, and correspondingly, inconceivability to imply metaphysical impossibility, only under certain conditions. Roughly, the link holds only when we are conceiving of the things involved in terms of their

---

[20] The main reason for this is that the conceivability of consciousness without the physical doesn't clearly refute functionalism, as functionalists may grant it's possible for consciousness to be realized by a non-physical system, even though it's actually physically realized. What functionalists cannot grant, however, is that it's possible for the physical realizer of a conscious system to exist without consciousness, as the zombie argument claims. But the disembodiment argument might still have some advantages, and versions of it have been defended by, e.g., Kripke (1980), Gertler (2007), Goff (2010), and Swinburne (2013).

[21] Possibility in principle (and hence metaphysically possibility understood according to this description) could be understood as more restrictive than logical or conceptual possibility: e.g., things like "an object with infinite parts," "the number 2 not existing," or "a color brighter than yellow but not white" could be regarded as impossible in principle (and hence metaphysically impossible) but still logically or conceptually possible. The most important thing, however, is that metaphysical possibility is much broader than nomological possibility.

real nature (Nida-Rümelin 2006; Goff 2017), as opposed to in terms of how they superficially appear, or in terms of other contingent (i.e., inessential or coincidental) or imprecise characteristics.[22]

For example, for someone who conceives of a triangle superficially or very imprecisely (because they have not studied geometry), it could be conceivable that its angles don't sum to 180 degrees, even though this is metaphysically impossible (assuming Euclidian space). But for someone who knows and understands all the characteristics of triangles and thinks about them in terms of their real nature, it should be inconceivable that their angles don't sum to 180 degrees, and it could be concluded from this that this is also metaphysically impossible. When it comes to consciousness, we also seem to know its real nature, as its nature consists in *what it's like* for us and this we seem to have direct access to. Therefore, (in)conceivability should be a guide to (im)possibility for consciousness in the same way that it is for geometrical objects, for example (for sufficiently qualified geometricians).

In order to make the final step from the metaphysical possibility of zombies to the falsity of physicalism, the argument also presupposes that if two things A and B are identical or A is constituted by B, then it's metaphysically impossible for B to exist without A (as influentially noted by Kripke (1980) for the case of identity, and the case of constitution is closely related). For example, if the statue David is constituted by a piece of marble in a certain shape, it's metaphysically impossible (i.e., impossible regardless of what the laws of nature may be) for that piece of marble to exist in that shape without the statue David also existing.[23] In the same way, if consciousness is constituted by a physical state – as physicalism claims – it should be metaphysically impossible for that physical state to exist without consciousness. But, according to the zombie argument, this is perfectly conceivable and hence metaphysically possible, meaning that physicalism is false.

1.4.3 The Explanatory Argument

The explanatory argument claims that consciousness can't be explained in physical terms; therefore, consciousness is not physical. This kind of argument goes back to Gottfried Wilhelm Leibniz (*Monadology*, paragraph 17), who asks

---

[22] This is roughly equivalent to saying that the link holds when things are considered under concepts that are "complete and adequate" (Descartes as quoted in Gertler 2007), *comprehensive* (Gertler 2007), *transparent* (Goff 2011, 2017), or whose primary and secondary intensions coincide (Chalmers 2009).

[23] It would also be possible for the statue David to be constituted by more than the piece of marble, e.g., by being made by a certain artist, and if so the piece of marble would not alone metaphysically necessitate David, but here we assume it is constituted solely by the marble. It's also possible for David to be multiply realizable, i.e., that it could have been made by, e.g., a different piece of marble, or by bronze. But existence of any one of these possible realizers still metaphysically necessitates the existence of David.

us to imagine a conscious system (i.e., one that "thinks, feels and has perception") large enough for us to walk into and inspect (as though it were a mill –
hence the argument is known as Leibniz' mill). Leibniz claims that no matter
how much we learned about the system and its parts, we could never find
anything to "explain a perception."

One might think modern neuroscience has improved upon this situation.
However, as Chalmers has argued (1995, 1996) (see also Levine 1983 and
Strawson 1994 for similar considerations), modern neuroscience and other
relevant sciences still aren't able to fully explain consciousness, at least not
by means of any of their standard methods.

The standard methods of neuroscience are sufficient to solve what Chalmers
calls *the easy problems* of consciousness. The easy problems consist in explaining the functions associated with consciousness (such as the ability to register
and process information about the environment, generating intelligent behavior,
and so on). To explain a function, all one has to do is identify a mechanism able
to perform or implement the function. And neuroscience has identified physical
mechanisms behind a number of important functions of consciousness (such as
the production of behavior and the capacity to process information, as already
outlined above), and it seems plausible that all the functions of consciousness
can eventually be fully explained in the same way.

But neuroscience has no method for solving what Chalmers calls *the hard
problem* of consciousness. The hard problem consists in explaining why phenomenal consciousness accompanies any of these functions, or how phenomenal consciousness arises from any physical processes at all (i.e., why aren't we
all zombies, in the sense of the conceivability argument)? When it comes to
phenomenal consciousness, it seems neuroscience can discover *correlations*
between phenomenal states and conscious states – for example, that the feeling
of depression is correlated with low serotonin, or seeing red with some activity
in the visual cortex. It might also identify what all the physical correlates of any
conscious state have in common – for example, that they are characterized by
high amounts of integrated information, as per the Integrated Information
Theory, or that they are connected to a global neuronal workspace, as per the
Global Workspace Theory, which are two leading general theories of consciousness in current neuroscience (the former will be discussed more detail in
Section 4). But neuroscience cannot explain why these correlations hold: why
couldn't we have, for example, low serotonin but no feeling of depression (but
rather, say a feeling of happiness or an experience of red), or high integrated
information but no consciousness at all?

According to Chalmers, there is a principled reason why neuroscience is
limited to finding mere correlations rather than full explanations, namely that its

standard methods consist in finding *reductive* explanations, that is, explanations of phenomena in terms of the underlying physical parts or processes that make them up. But the only phenomena that can be reductively explained are *functions or structures*: functions can be reductively explained by finding physical mechanisms that perform them (as when solving the easy problems), and structures can be reductively explained by identifying the parts that compose them and the relations between them (e.g., a crystal, which can be understood as a structure, can be explained by identifying the molecules that compose it and the chemical bonds that hold between them). Phenomenal consciousness, in contrast, is not a mere function or structure: it may *have* functions and structure (e.g., a visual experience may have the function of informing us about the environment, and the structure of containing a distribution of different colors), but there is more to it than this (namely, *what it's like*). Therefore, it can never be reductively explained. This argument, which can be regarded as a sub-argument of the explanatory argument, is known as *the structure and function argument.*

At this point, physicalists might invoke the argument from mind–brain correlations, according to which the correlations between conscious states and brain states can be explained by simply assuming that conscious states are constituted by their correlated physical states. But according to the explanatory argument, one cannot simply assume that conscious states are constituted by physical states, it must be *shown* that they are. To offer a reductive explanation is just to show how consciousness is physically constituted, and this is what the explanatory argument claims is impossible.

Physicalists may also invoke the argument from previous explanatory successes of science, according to which other phenomena that once seemed impossible to physically explain eventually were. Chalmers responds to this argument that all phenomena that have previously been reductively explained have been functional or structural phenomena. For example, diseases can be defined (roughly) by the function of making people sick, and life has been scientifically defined as a set of functions including metabolism, growth, homeostasis, reproduction, and so on. They can thereby be reductively explained by appeal to mechanisms such as germs (for diseases), or genes and DNA (for life). That a number of functional or structural phenomena have been physically explained gives us no reason to expect that a non-functional and non-structural, and thus entirely different, phenomenon such as phenomenal consciousness can be physically explained as well.

Note that the explanatory argument only claims that phenomenal consciousness can't be *reductively* explained, or explained in *physical* terms. Phenomenal consciousness could still be explained *non-reductively*, or in *non-physical* terms, but this would result in a non-physicalist theory.

1.4.4 The Epistemic Gap – and Physicalist Responses

The knowledge, conceivability, and explanatory argument have something important in common. They each point out a disconnect between our *knowledge* or *concepts* of phenomenal consciousness and our knowledge or concepts of the physical, and conclude from this that phenomenal consciousness *itself* is not physical. As Chalmers (2003) sums it up, they each point out an *epistemic gap* – a gap within what we can know or conceive ("epistemic" means regarding knowledge) – and conclude from this that there is an *ontological gap* – a gap in reality or between what *is* ("ontological" means regarding what there is or what reality fundamentally consists of). The arguments could therefore be jointly referred to as *the arguments from the epistemic gap*.

Physicalists have offered numerous and varied responses to these arguments (for an overview of the main strategies, see Chalmers 2003). In general, however, physicalists may seem primarily motivated, not by specific errors perceived in the arguments *against* physicalism (in fact, some physicalists admit to finding them fairly compelling), but rather by how the arguments *for* physicalism seem so strong. The argument from physical causal closure, especially, carries much weight (as we saw, the explanatory argument against physicalism may cast some doubt on both the argument from mind–brain correlations and the argument from previous successes). Many philosophers find it far more plausible that there is *some* error in the arguments against physicalism – even if we can't be sure exactly what the error is – than that phenomenal consciousness is epiphenomenal, an overdeterminer, or violates physical causal closure, as would follow from rejecting physicalism according to this argument.

Non-physicalists therefore need to answer the arguments *for* physicalism, the argument from physical causal closure in particular, in addition to offering arguments against it. From the next section onward, we will see how each of the main non-physicalist theories do this. But first, let us consider some further arguments against physicalism based on consciousness' features of intentionality and unity.

1.4.5 Arguments Based on Intentionality

Intentionality (recall, the way conscious states can be *about* things in the world) can also be considered a problem for physicalism. One of the most influential arguments to this effect is based on *the rule-following problem* first raised by Ludwig Wittgenstein. According to this problem, when we consider any sequence of items, such as "1, 3, 5, 7 ...," it will always be compatible with a number of different rules, such as "add 2" (if so, the next item will be 9) or "add 2 three times, then subtract 2 three times" (if so, the next item will be 5) or "add 2 three times, then repeat the same number forever" (if so, the next item will be 7). That is, we can never infer which rule is being followed from the output of the rule alone.

In the same way, it does not seem possible to infer the meaning of an intentional state, such as a thought, or an expression of it, such as a word, from studying its physical manifestations alone. Quine (1960) argues that we can't tell from someone's behavior of uttering "rabbit" only in the presence of rabbits that this word refers to rabbits rather than, for example, undetached rabbit parts, which will always be present at the same time. Kripke (1982) argues that no physical facts determine whether someone apparently performing addition is not actually performing *quaddition*, which, just like addition, outputs the sum when applied to numbers up to 57 (or some other arbitrary number), but when applied to higher numbers always outputs 5, or relatedly, whether by the word "plus" they mean plus (in the sense of addition) or *quus* (in the sense of *quaddition*).

One might sum this up by saying that there is an *epistemic gap* from physical facts to intentional facts about meaning, in that the latter can't be deduced from or explained by physical facts. Some, including Quine and Kripke, conclude from this that there are no determinate facts about meaning (such as about whether by the word "plus" we mean plus or *quus*) – because they don't think any mental facts could determine meaning either. But others hold that there clearly are facts about meaning, and if physical facts don't determine (or leave an epistemic gap to) them, facts about meaning must be regarded as non-physical.[24]

A typical response to this problem is to argue that although meaning isn't physically determined in any simple or obvious way, it could be physically determined in more subtle or complex ways. For example, a number of attempts have been made at *naturalizing* intentionality – where by "naturalizing" is meant roughly the same as accounting for in physical terms – in terms of the physical abilities of conscious beings to track objects or features in their environment (Millikan 1984; Dretske 1988; Fodor 1990), that many regard as promising.

In view of this, some non-physicalists accept that intentionality can be physically explained, but still deny that phenomenality can (e.g., Kim 2005).[25] One reason to treat intentionality differently in this respect is that, as we have seen, phenomenality appears non-functional and non-structural and arguably only functional and structural phenomena can be physically explained. But intentionality could be regarded as purely structural, because it may seem to consist mainly

---

[24] E.g., Ross (1992) and Goff (2012). Some proponents of the phenomenal intentionality theories, to be discussed shortly (e.g., Strawson 2008a), have also implicitly endorsed this argument by taking intentionality to be grounded in phenomenality and phenomenality to be non-physical, but they often treat these issues separately and therefore don't explicitly present the whole argument.

[25] Kim is widely known as a physicalist, but in his 2005, he (somewhat reluctantly) accepts a kind of property dualism.

in a special type of relation (the "aboutness" relation) between consciousness and things in the world. Hence, there is less of a principled obstacle to physically explaining it.

Other non-physicalists hold that while intentionality cannot be fully explained in physical terms it can still be fully explained in phenomenal terms, or alternatively, in a combination of phenomenal and physical terms, as per what is known as *phenomenal intentionality* theories (Horgan and Tienson 2002; Strawson 2008a; Kriegel 2013; Mendelovici and Bourget 2014). According to such theories, *what it's like* to be a given person – and this may include distinctively intentional or cognitive phenomenal qualities, such as feelings of intention, will, understanding, and so on – fully determines their intentional states, or (on some versions) determines them together with physical facts about various relations to the environment.

If intentionality is constituted either by the physical alone (as per attempts at naturalizing intentionality), the phenomenal alone or a combination of the phenomenal and physical (as per phenomenal intentionality theories), it poses no distinct problem for physicalism. For it to pose a distinct problem, intentionality must itself appear fundamental, or constituted by neither the physical nor the phenomenal, and this view is less often defended.

1.4.6 Arguments Based on Unity

The way consciousness seems distinctively unified has also given rise to arguments against physicalism. Descartes made an argument of this sort (*Meditations*, VI), according to which the mind is indivisible, whereas all physical bodies are divisible; therefore, the mind is non-physical.

More recent arguments claim, somewhat similarly, that the unity of consciousness must be accounted for by a *subject* distinct from the experiences it's having, and subjects are simple and unified, but nothing physical is simple and unified in the same way (or at least no complex physical systems – fundamental particles may be simple and unified, but the argument tends to assume that subjects of experience couldn't be constituted by single particles). Therefore, subjects are not physical (this or similar arguments have been defended by, e.g., Lowe 1996; Nida-Rümelin 2007; Hasker 2010; Barnett 2010; Swinburne 2013). Since, according to this argument, unity is a feature of subjects that are distinct from their phenomenal experiences, unity poses a problem for physicalism distinct from the problem of phenomenality.

As already mentioned, however, many philosophers, non-physicalists included, hold that the unity of consciousness can be accounted for by relations amongst phenomenal qualities themselves, rather than by a distinct subject, as per the deflationary view of subjects (Section 1.1; see also Strawson 2008b; Dainton 2010 for defenses of different versions of the deflationary view). If the unity of consciousness is just a relation between phenomenal qualities, then it may fall within the same category, and be explained in the same way, as these phenomenal qualities, and unity would not pose a distinct problem for physicalism after all (for other criticisms of unity arguments, see Bayne 2018b).

A related argument is the argument from identity across time. According to this argument, the same conscious being can exist at different points in time: for example, you now are the same person as you yesterday or you five years ago, and will be the same person tomorrow or in five years. This relation is not a matter of degree: for any conscious being in the past or future, you are either *absolutely* identical to them or not at all: you cannot be *partially* identical to anyone. But the physical body (including the brain) is not like this: your body tomorrow, for example, will contain at least a few different atoms and have various other physical differences (such as a few new hairs on your head, slightly different neuron configurations, etc.), and so is only partially identical to your body now. If you are absolutely identical to yourself in the past or future, then, it has to be in virtue of something non-physical that stays exactly the same, such as being the same non-physical subject (Nida-Rümelin 2009; Swinburne 2013). Typical objections to this argument, however, include that perhaps we shouldn't really take ourselves to be absolutely identical over time (Parfit 1971), or that absolute identity can in fact be accounted for physically, or in terms of mental *properties*, rather than a mental substance (see Olson 2003).

In the following sections, we will consider how the main non-physicalist theories can accommodate each of the arguments for and against physicalism mentioned so far. But for some of the arguments, there are no significant differences between the theories. When it comes to unity arguments against physicalism, we will see that some non-physicalist theories (such as substance dualism, subjective idealism, and emergent panpsychism) may be better able to accommodate them, and can therefore be seen as having an advantage – but only if one rejects the deflationary view of subjects, which many non-physicalists accept. When it comes to the arguments against physicalism based on phenomenality and intentionality, all non-physicalist theories can be regarded as equally accommodating – since they all agree that phenomenality is non-physical, and intentionality is widely regarded as being constituted either by phenomenality, the physical, or a combination thereof (in addition, they would also seem compatible with positing intentionality as fundamental alongside phenomenality).

The most significant differences are found in how the theories can respond to the arguments *for* physicalism, that is, the arguments from mind–brain correlations, previous explanatory successes, and physical causal closure – the latter, as discussed, being especially important – as well as the problems and objections that apply to each non-physicalist theory specifically, so this will be the main focus of discussion.

2 Dualism

Dualism can be defined as the view that (1) the mental (including phenomenal properties, but perhaps also intentionality, subjects or other mental properties or entities) and the physical are both fundamental (i.e., neither is constituted by the other nor by anything else), and (2) the mental and the physical stand in a *causal* relation to each other.

The causal connection between the mental and the physical can be understood in terms of fundamental psychophysical laws, forces, powers, or dispositions. For example, just like we have *physical laws* of gravity, electromagnetism, and so on, dualists may claim we have *psychophysical laws* (i.e., laws that connect the psychological, understood as the mental, and the physical) according to which certain physical states produce and have effects on consciousness, and conscious states may in turn (given interactionism or overdetermination) produce physical effects. Or, it might be claimed that, in addition to the fundamental physical forces (such as the electromagnetic or gravitational force) there is a physical force by which matter produces or affects consciousness and perhaps also a mental force by which consciousness affects matter. For simplicity, we will mostly talk about psychophysical laws, but these laws could be interpreted either as fundamental or as descriptions of behavior that follows from fundamental forces, powers, or dispositions.

2.1 Substance Dualism, Property Dualism, and Emergentism

The traditional version of dualism, defended by Descartes, is *substance dualism*. Substance dualism regards the mental and the physical as two different substances, that is, two different fundamental kinds of things or stuff. *Property dualism*, in contrast, regards the mental and the physical as two fundamental kinds of properties, which can belong to (or inhere in) the same substance, that is, the same thing or stuff. The possibility of property dualism may have first been considered by John Locke, who pondered the possibility of "thinking matter" as an alternative to Descartes' thinking non-material substances (*An Essay Concerning Human Understanding*, IV.3.6).

Property dualism seems more parsimonious (i.e., simpler, in the sense of positing fewer things or kinds of things) than substance dualism. It may also posit that phenomenal properties must inhere in a physical substance or thing (or a thing that also has physical properties), and thereby explain why consciousness depends on the brain and can't exist disembodied. Scientifically oriented philosophers therefore tend to prefer property dualism (e.g., Chalmers 1996, though he is also open to substance dualism [Chalmers 2010a, p. 139, fn. 36], and Kim 2005).

Substance dualism, on the other hand, is more compatible with the arguments from unity, according to which the unity of consciousness (as well as perhaps identity across time) must be accounted for by a distinct subject (as opposed to a mere "bundling" of experiences amongst themselves), because such a subject would seem equivalent to a substance. In other words, the unity arguments can be regarded as supporting substance dualism in particular, as opposed to dualism or non-physicalism in general (most of the philosophers cited in the previous section as defending unity arguments also take them to support substance dualism – though, as discussed in later sections, some versions of other non-physicalist theories seem compatible with them as well).

Another advantage of substance dualism is its compatibility with Descartes' version of the conceivability argument, the argument from disembodiment, according to which consciousness is conceivable without the body or the external world. This supports the idea that mental properties can inhere in a purely mental substance. Religiously oriented philosophers may also see the possibility of disembodied minds, more clearly allowed for by substance dualism, as an advantage, as it may allow for an afterlife, though there are also philosophers who support substance dualism on purely non-religious grounds (e.g., Nida-Rümelin 2007).

Property dualists could respond, as already mentioned in Section 1.1, that the unity of consciousness can be accounted for without a distinct subject, by adopting the deflationary view. The conceivability of consciousness without anything else could be taken to show that properties don't need to inhere in a substance at all – perhaps they could rather exist as *tropes*, that is, pure, free-floating instances of properties (see Maurin 2018). Or, property dualists could take it to show that it's metaphysically possible (i.e., logically possible or possible in principle) for phenomenal consciousness to inhere in a substance that does not also have physical properties, but maintain that this is still nomologically impossible (i.e., incompatible with the actual psychophysical laws).

It should also be noted that some take property dualism to imply substance dualism (Schneider 2012; Strawson 2006a), or to share most of the same problems (Lycan 2013; Zimmerman 2010), so the distinction between them may not be as important as often thought.

Property dualism should be distinguished from *non-reductive physicalism*. Non-reductive physicalism (e.g., Davidson 1980) claims that phenomenal properties (or types) are not identical to physical properties (or types), but it still takes particular instances (or tokens) of phenomenal properties to be fully constituted by instances (or tokens) of physical properties, whereas property dualism takes both phenomenal properties and their instances (or tokens) to be non-physical and fundamental.

Also note that dualism of any sort that takes consciousness to be causally produced by the brain or other physical configurations – as opposed to having some other origin, such as being directly created or transferred into the physical world by God, as per some religious or pre-modern dualist views – can be described as *emergentism*. But the term emergentism is also widely used to describe various kinds of physicalism, as well as views indeterminate between physicalism and dualism, so one should be careful to avoid misunderstandings around this term.

2.2 The Interaction Problem

A traditional objection to dualism is known as the interaction problem. This problem was raised by Descartes' correspondent Princess Elisabeth of Bohemia, and claims that it's not *intelligible* (i.e., cannot be explained or understood) how the mental and physical interact, if they are considered two different substances.

This argument is different from the argument from physical causal closure, according to which interaction between the physical and the non-physical conflicts with our scientific evidence. According to the interaction problem, interaction between the physical and the non-physical can be ruled out for a philosophical reason largely independent of specific scientific evidence.

The standard response to this problem is that interaction between physical causes and effects is not really intelligible either (e.g., Chalmers 2003, p. 125). Hume famously argued that we cannot explain or understand the connection between any causes and effects, as all we perceive is causes being *followed* by effects, but nothing that binds them together, such as powers or forces. If interaction between physical causes is not intelligible, then interaction between physical and non-physical causes should not be required to be either.

But not everyone accepts Hume's view that causation is completely unintelligible. For example, one might assume that causation involves transfer of energy, where energy is understood roughly as per current physics. On the one hand, it could be argued that energy can't be transferred between physical and non-physical substances, because energy is physical and everything that has physical energy must itself be physical. But it can be objected that it's not clear why energy can't be regarded as a neutral rather than physical property, or why non-physical things can't have physical energy (see Montero 2006; note that these points are also relevant to why the principle of conservation of energy is insufficient to establish the principle of physical causal closure, as discussed in Section 1.3.2).

But what if energy is not something things have or possess, but rather something they are made of or constituted by? In physics, it is sometimes said that everything *is* (rather than *has*) a form of energy. That energy is something things are constituted by may also be supported by the equivalence of mass and energy (i.e., Einstein's $e=mc^2$), and the fact that particles with no energy cannot exist. If things are made of energy, and causation requires transfer of energy, then causation requires transferring a part or constituent of oneself. And a non-physical substance can't receive a physical part or constituent without becoming partially physical, and vice versa (Mørch ms).

In response to this version of the interaction problem, dualists could argue against either the claim that things *are* rather than *have* energy (see, e.g., Fernflores 2019 for different interpretations of the mass–energy equivalence, some of which do not imply this) or the claim that causation requires transfer of energy (e.g., some take it to be refuted by causation by omission, such as the death of a plant being caused by *not* being watered, which involves no transfer of energy).

2.3 Dualism and the Arguments for Physicalism

How can dualism respond to the arguments for physicalism? The argument from mind–brain correlations and the argument from previous explanatory successes can be answered quite simply. Against the argument from mind–brain correlations, dualists may grant both that physicalism is simpler and more elegant than dualism, and that we should always prefer the simplest and most elegant explanation, but only among those explanations compatible with the data – and the epistemic gap between the mental and the physical is a datum incompatible with physicalism, but compatible with dualism.

Against the argument from previous explanatory successes, dualists can invoke the point that consciousness is non-structural (as per the structure and function argument), subjective (as opposed to objective), or otherwise fundamentally different from any previously explained phenomena, and one cannot generalize from phenomena of one kind to phenomena of a fundamentally different kind.

The argument from physical causal closure poses a greater challenge, according to which non-physicalists must choose between epiphenomenalism, over-determination and denial of physical causal closure. Given dualism, these seem like the only options (as we will see later, other non-physicalist theories may have others). Dualists must therefore argue that at least one of these options is not as bad as physicalists make them out to be.

2.3.1 Epiphenomenalist Dualism

Given epiphenomenalist dualism, the psychophysical laws connecting consciousness and the physical go in one direction only: there are laws according to which physical causes produce mental effects, but no laws according to which mental causes produce physical effects.

Epiphenomenalists generally admit that their view is unattractive in a number of ways, but argue that it's still less unattractive than the alternatives. More specifically, they tend to take both physicalism and interactionism to be refuted, or at least rendered highly implausible, by the epistemic gap and physical causal closure respectively. The arguments against epiphenomenalism, in contrast, don't refute it nor render it nearly as implausible – at best, they point out reasons to dislike it or ways in which it's counterintuitive (i.e., goes against what we find natural to believe), which are not valid reasons to reject it (Chalmers 1996, p. 160). In addition, epiphenomenalists must endorse some of the arguments against other non-physicalist views (to be discussed in Sections 3 and 4) as more powerful than the arguments against epiphenomenalism.

The most basic argument against epiphenomenalism is that phenomenal states clearly appear to cause physical actions. Epiphenomenalists can simply respond that not everything that appears true is actually true, and in view of the evidence for physical causal closure, we should regard this appearance as false. One might object that, in that case, we might as well deny that consciousness exists in the first place, because our evidence for this is mainly that it appears to exist. Epiphenomenalists can respond that consciousness appears more strongly to exist than it appears to produce physical effects, or that appearances regarding the existence of consciousness are more (perhaps even absolutely) trustworthy in view of the direct access we have to our own consciousness, but this direct access does not extend to what our consciousness may or may not cause.

A second argument claims that epiphenomenalism is far less elegant than both physicalism and other kinds of dualism, because it posits consciousness as an idle "nomological dangler" (Smart 1959), rather than something properly integrated into the physical world. However, if the more elegant theories are refuted (physicalism by the epistemic gap and interactionism by physical causal closure), this is a moot point.

A third argument claims that epiphenomenalism is pragmatically untenable, or renders our lives meaningless practically speaking. This sentiment is powerfully expressed by Jerry Fodor[26]: "... if it isn't literally true that my wanting is causally responsible for my reaching, and my itching is causally responsible for my scratching, and my believing is causally responsible for my saying ..., if none of that is literally true, then practically everything I believe about anything is false and it's the end of the world" (1990, p. 156).

Fodor here notes the radical implications of epiphenomenalism for how we look at our own lives. If our mental states have no physical effects, then not only do we (understood as mental beings) lack *free* will, that is, the ability to freely cause physical actions – as philosophers routinely worry about – we actually lack any will at all, that is, the ability to cause physical actions either freely or not.[27] This turns us into passive spectators of our own lives – like the audiences of a movie, rather than actors in the drama. This would deprive our lives of much, if not most, of the meaning we ordinarily take it to have.

It could be objected that epiphenomenalists need not take mental states in general to have no physical effects, because some mental states, such as intentional states, may be physical even though others, such as phenomenal states, are non-physical. However, as discussed, many non-physicalists take intentionality to be non-physical as well. Furthermore, if our intentions can produce actions, but our phenomenal states can't produce intentions (e.g., the feeling of love can't cause you to intend to hug someone) it still puts strong limitations on our agency.

Epiphenomenalists may still respond that perhaps our lives just aren't as meaningful as we think, or at least not meaningful in the way we usually think. In other words, that this is one of the features of epiphenomenalism we might not like, but that doesn't mean it's not true.

A fourth argument against epiphenomenalism claims that it renders it inexplicable how consciousness could have evolved, because if epiphenomenalism is true, consciousness is inert and useless, and useless features don't evolve (Eccles and Popper 1977; Popper 1978). In response, epiphenomenalists have noted that useless features may evolve as by-products of useful features, and

---

[26] Fodor here reacts to epiphenomenalism of a sort that would arguably result from non-reductive physicalism (as discussed in Section 2.1), but the same point also applies to dualist epiphenomenalism. Also note that some epiphenomenalists defend their view on the basis the claim that non-reductive physicalism, which is arguably the most plausible version of physicalism, also implies epiphenomenalism (see Robb and Heil 2013, section 6). It can be responded, however, that this kind of epiphenomenalism is avoidable or less severe (Robb and Heil 2013, sections 6.4, 6.5).

[27] More precisely, epiphenomenalism may allow us the ability to cause (freely or unfreely) *mental* actions (e.g., I might mentally intend to imagine a red circle or think of random number and have this mental intention cause these mental results), because physical causal closure only precludes the mental from having physical effects. But if we can't produce physical actions very little of what we usually take to be our agency is preserved.

given epiphenomenalism conscious states could be by-products of useful brain states (Broad 1925; Jackson 1982).

One might still wonder, however, why specific conscious states, such as pain and pleasure, have evolved as by-products of specific physical states and not other ones (James 1890, pp. 143–144). For example, why has pain (or feelings of discomfort) evolved as a by-product of harmful physical states or processes, such as burning or suffocation, and pleasure (or feelings of comfort) as a by-product of beneficial states or processes, such as eating or breathing – rather than the other way around? In other words, why are conscious states such as pain and pleasure correlated with physical states that seem *fitting* or *appropriate*, in the way that avoidance-causing physical states seem to be fitting for pain, and attraction-causing physical states seem to be fitting for pleasure?

If epiphenomenalism is false, and pain causes avoidance behavior, it follows, for example, that creatures for whom harmful states (such as burning) are (fittingly) correlated with pain will avoid what's harmful and thereby be selected for by evolution. Creatures for whom harmful states are correlated (unfittingly) with pleasure, on the other hand, will be attracted to and pursue what's harmful to them, and thereby be selected against by evolution.

But if pain has no causal effects – as per epiphenomenalism – switching around pain and pleasure would make no difference to behavior and thus be ignored by natural selection. For example, a creature for whom harmful states cause pain might still pursue them and so be selected against, and a creature for whom harmful states cause pleasure might still avoid them and be selected for. To explain why (in most cases) pain is correlated with harmful states (as well as pleasure with beneficial states, for which the situation would be analogous), epiphenomenalism must be rejected – or so the argument goes.

In response to this argument, it has been argued that non-epiphenomenalist theories, such as interactionism and physicalism, actually face the same problem (Robinson 2007; Corabi 2014). This is because epiphenomenalism can in fact explain the fitting correlations (assuming natural selection) by positing one-way psychophysical laws according to which pain is a by-product of avoidance-causing physical states in particular, and pleasure is a by-product of attraction-causing physical states in particular. Granted, this leads to a further explanatory question of why we have these particular one-way psychophysical laws rather than other ones. But to explain the fitting correlations, interactionism must posit specific two-way psychophysical laws according to which pain causes avoidance and pleasure causes pursuit in particular, whereas physicalism must posit specific psychophysical constitution relations according to which pain is constituted by avoidance-causing physical states, and pleasure is constituted by attraction-causing physical states in particular. These two-way laws or constitution relations are just as much in need of explanation as epiphenomenalism's one-way laws.[28] If this is correct, epiphenomenalism has no unique explanatory disadvantage after all.

Epiphenomenalism can also be confronted with other correlations between conscious states and physical behavior that seem fitting or appropriate in a way the view arguably can't explain. For example, not only is it a mystery, given epiphenomenalism, why pain happens to be a by-product of physical states that cause avoidance (rather than attraction) behavior, one might also wonder why the phenomenal experience of red is a by-product of physical states that dispose us to utter "I'm seeing red" (rather than "I'm seeing blue," or to exhibit some completely different behavior such as jumping or dancing). Or, if intentional states are also regarded as non-physical, one might wonder why intentions to, for example, raise one's arm, are by-products of physical states that tend to produce arm-raising (rather than, e.g., leg-raising or no action) (see Cutter and Crummett [forthcoming] for further examples of such correlations, or instances of *psychophysical harmony*, as they call it). Epiphenomenalists can respond to these arguments in the same way as above: non-epiphenomenalist theories, such as physicalism and interactionism, can explain these correlations only by positing specific two-way psychophysical laws or identity/constitution relations that are just as unexpected and improbable as the one-way laws epiphenomenalists may posit to explain the same correlations.[29]

A related problem, known as *the paradox of phenomenal judgment* (Chalmers 1996), is that if our judgments about our experiences (such as "I'm experiencing red") are not caused by the experiences themselves, as epiphenomenalists maintain, these judgments will be unjustified, because it's typically held that judgments are justified only if they are somehow causally influenced by what they are about (this is known as the causal theory of justification). This is a problem in and of itself, and also because epiphenomenalism is itself

---

[28] One might object, on behalf of physicalism, that constitution relations are metaphysically necessary, not contingent (i.e., possibly different) like psychophysical laws, and therefore don't require explanation, but see Corabi (2014) and Mørch (2017a) for a reply. Epiphenomenalists could also accept this objection and be content with generalizing the problem to interactionism and other kinds of non-physicalism, as they might take physicalism to be refuted by the epistemic gap anyway.

[29] Does this mean the fittingness of such correlations can't be explained at all? I have proposed that the fittingness can be explained by appeal, not to any particular theory of consciousness, but rather by a theory of causation called the phenomenal powers view (Mørch 2017a, 2020). This view is not compatible with epiphenomenalism, but it's also hard to reconcile with physicalism, so if this explanation works, it can be used as an argument against both physicalism and epiphenomenalism, rather than against epiphenomenalism only. Other explanations (that invoke, e.g., God, or fundamental values in the universe) of these as well as other kinds of seemingly fitting psychophysical correlations can be found in Goff (2018) and Cutter and Crummett (forthcoming).

a judgment about our experiences ("all experiences are non-physical and epiphenomenal"). It seems to follow that epiphenomenalism itself lacks justification and the view can be regarded as self-undermining.

In response to this problem, Chalmers has argued (1996, 2010b) that our phenomenal judgments (understood as mental thoughts rather than physical utterances) are different from other sorts of judgments in that they need not be *caused* by what they are about. Rather, when we have a thought or make a judgment about an experience, the experience can be understood as a *part* or *constituent* of the thought or judgment. It follows that these judgments can be justified without any causal connections (i.e., it offers non-causal theory of justification). It can also be argued that other non-physicalist theories should adopt the same theory of phenomenal judgments, among other reasons because it may seem necessary to account for our direct and immediate access to our own consciousness, which most non-physicalists hold that we have. Any objections one may have to this theory would therefore be a problem not just for epiphenomenalism but for other non-physicalist theories as well.

The most serious problems for epiphenomenalism, may therefore be those based on conflict with appearances, inelegance, and pragmatic consequences – which may not decisively refute it, but still put it at a clear disadvantage if there are other views that can avoid them (without incurring other at least equally serious problems).

2.3.2 Overdetermination Dualism

According to overdetermination dualism, the psychophysical laws go in both directions: physical states produce conscious states, and conscious states in turn produce physical effects such as behavior. However, conscious states will produce the exact same physical effects as the brain states they are correlated with. Our physical behavior will thus have two causes, a conscious state and a brain state, where each cause would have been sufficient on its own – in the same way that someone's death can be doubly caused by a shot to the head and a simultaneous shot to the heart, where each shot would have been deadly on its own.

The overdetermination will also need to be *systematic*, which is to say that our behavior always and without exception has a sufficient physical cause in addition to its mental cause, and the physical cause will never fail such that the mental cause gets a chance to cause the behavior on its own (i.e., there has to be some mechanism such that if the physical cause fails, then so does the mental cause), as this would break physical causal closure.

Overdetermination dualism thus shares with epiphenomenalism the advantage of being compatible with physical causal closure. It also shares the disadvantage of being not very elegant. But unlike epiphenomenalism, it allows the mental to affect the physical.

Still, few philosophers prefer overdetermination over epiphenomenalism. The main reason is that it seems completely inexplicable why conscious states would, systematically and without exception, cause the exact same effects as the physical states they are correlated with. There is no reason to expect the psychophysical laws (connecting conscious states to behavior) to mirror the physical laws (connecting brain states to behavior) in this way, and since there are so many different ways they could possibly diverge, it seems extremely implausible that they would mirror each other simply by coincidence.[30] Overdetermination dualism itself is therefore generally regarded as just as implausible (though see Mills 1996 for a defense).

2.3.3 Interactionist Dualism

Interactionist dualism posits two-way psychophysical laws, according to which consciousness and the physical world mutually influence each other, where the physical effects of mental causes have no sufficient physical cause and are thus not overdetermined (except perhaps on rare occasions by coincidence, as opposed to systematically and without exception, as per overdetermination dualism). Consciousness may either cause physical behavior all by itself, or together with physical causes in such a way that both contribute but neither are sufficient – in the same way a forest fire can be caused by both drought and a lightning strike, where if one were missing the fire would not occur.

By denying that physical behavior has sufficient physical causes, interactionism is straightforwardly incompatible with physical causal closure. Interactionists must therefore argue that the evidence for this principle isn't as strong as we think, all things considered. Strategies for this can be divided into two types, those that invoke quantum mechanics and those that don't. We will begin with the latter.

As mentioned, the most important argument for physical causal closure is the argument from physiology, according to which there is no evidence of non-physical forces influencing the brain and body, and we are getting closer and closer to a complete physical explanation of all processes in the brain and body.

---

[30] Note that this problem is different from the problem (discussed in Section 2.3.1) of explaining the fittingness of various correlations between conscious states and physical bases with the right effects that can be raised for epiphenomenalism, but as discussed really generalizes to other views as well, including overdetermination dualism. Given overdetermination, then not only are the psychophysical laws fitting in terms of connecting conscious states with physical states with the right effects, they are also fitting in terms of mirroring the physical laws, and other views have no analogue of this latter problem.

There are, however, philosophers and scientists who disagree, at least if the physical explanation is understood as one that invokes only the laws of *micro-physics* (i.e., the physics of entities or properties at the smallest level or reality, such as particles).

Strong physical emergentism is the view that genuinely novel properties or behaviors arise in complex macrophysical objects such as the brain, which can't be accounted for by the laws of microphysics alone, but must rather be accounted for by fundamental laws of higher-level sciences such as chemistry, biology, or neurology. Philosophers who defend such strong emergence within the physical, or at least regard it as an open possibility in view of the current state of evidence, include Cartwright (1983), Boogerd et al. (2005), and Gillett (2016) (see also Broad 1925 for a classic defense). Interactionists could take such strongly emergent physical properties or behaviors to be caused by consciousness – at least when occurring in the brain.

Physicalists could retort that this is only a speculative possibility with no clear evidence to support it (McLaughlin 1992). They may also argue that strongly emergent physical properties or behavior, if actual, could still be explicable in terms of laws of physical sciences such as biology and neurology. Even if these sciences aren't part of *microphysics* (because their laws, given strong physical emergentism, fundamentally apply only at the macrolevel), they may count as a part of *physics* broadly speaking. Thus, strong emergence would not require explanation in non-physical terms (only in non-microphysical terms). Another issue is that most strong physical emergentists take strong physical emergence to occur in systems beyond the body and brain, such as molecules or cells (including non-human cells such as plant cells or bacteria). In view of this, dualists must either posit consciousness in all these systems – thereby approaching panpsychism – or explain why strong physical emergence has a non-physical, mental cause in the brain but a physical cause elsewhere (Mørch 2014).

Now for the responses based on quantum mechanics. Quantum mechanics describes physical systems by means of a wave function, according to which systems exist in a *superposition* between different states. For example, if the system is a particle, the wave function will describe it as superposed between many different positions and many different velocities. When we make a measurement, we will always find the particle in a definite location or with a definite velocity.[31] This is known as the *collapse* of the wave function (i.e., the reduction of its many possibilities to one). The *probability* of finding the particle in a particular position or with a particular velocity upon measurement can be

---

[31] But not both at once: if the position is measured and then the velocity, the position will go back into superposition – as per Heisenberg's uncertainty principle.

predicted from the wave function. But no matter how much information we gather – or at least *local* information about anything able to directly causally affect the particle, as per Bell's theorem of no local hidden variables – we can never predict the particular position or velocity the particle will collapse into with certainty. The outcomes of measurements of quantum systems thereby seem fundamentally *indeterministic*. Indeterminism is the view that some events are not fixed or necessitated by prior causes, laws of nature, or anything else, while *determinism* is the opposite view that all events *are* thus fixed or necessitated.

There are different interpretations of quantum mechanics, some of which preserve determinism by positing non-local hidden variables or that collapse actually never happens (e.g., Bohm's pilot-wave interpretation or Everett's many-worlds interpretation). But quantum mechanics can also be interpreted in ways that accept indeterminism and collapse. Interactionists have taken this to suggest a causal role for non-physical consciousness, either as influencing the outcome of collapse by deciding between or narrowing down the possibilities contained in the wave function, or by causing collapse but without necessarily influencing the outcome.

The idea that consciousness may play the role of influencing the outcome of quantum collapse has been seized upon not only by interactionist dualists (e.g., Eccles and Popper 1977) but also by libertarians about free will (e.g., Van Inwagen 1983; Kane 1985; Balaguer 2009). Libertarianism is the view that humans have freedom to choose between otherwise genuinely undecided (i.e., indeterministic) possibilities. It should be noted that interactionism does not imply libertarianism,[32] as the psychophysical laws governing interaction between consciousness and the physical world could be deterministic (thus securing that conscious beings have *will*, but not necessarily *free will*, as distinguished earlier). But the kind of interactionism that takes consciousness to affect the physical by influencing the outcome of quantum collapse (rather than in some other way) seems to at least strongly suggest libertarianism, since collapse is indeterministic.

Is it possible that non-physical consciousness influences the outcome of collapse? There are two main obstacles to this idea. The first is that indeterminism at the microlevel, such as a particle having an undetermined position, does not imply indeterminism at the macrolevel, that is, at the level of behavior or its precursors, such as it being undetermined whether a neuron is firing or not (and as a result, whether some action that would be triggered by this firing is performed or not). This is because even though the wave function does not

---

[32] Similarly, libertarianism does not imply interactionist dualism, but is compatible with it.

determine the properties of individual particles, it does determine the average or other statistical properties of large numbers of particles. For example, if the wave function assigns a 20 percent chance that an individual particle will be found in area X, then we can expect close to 20 percent of particles of the same type to be found in area X as we measure large numbers of them. Macrolevel states, such as whether a neuron is firing or an action is performed, will usually depend on average or other statistical properties of a large number of particles, and therefore be statistically determined.

Still, there are ways in which indeterminism could be possible at the macro-level after all. One possibility is that the collapse of single particles or other tiny systems within the brain can be amplified so as to lead to large scale effects, in a way similar[33] to the butterfly effect known from chaos theory (according to which a single butterfly flutter could be decisive in triggering a hurricane) (Koch 2009; Aaronson 2016; see also Jedlicka 2017 for a survey of the evidence for and against this hypothesis).

Another possibility is that macrolevel states (in this context, at the molecular level or higher, which is roughly the minimum threshold for being able to decisively influence action without relying on the kind of amplification just discussed) within the brain could themselves be superposed. This would require that these states achieve quantum *coherence*, which is roughly to be in a superposed and internally entangled state that is not destroyed by interference from the environment. Entanglement is a relation between different particles or objects where collapse of one instantly implies collapse of the other(s), regard-less of how far away from each other they are located, and where the outcomes are strictly correlated (e.g., if particle 1 collapses to "spin up," particle 2, which may be far away, must instantly collapse to "spin down"). A coherent macro-state constituted by entangled microstates of numerous particles will therefore behave as one superposed state. It is standardly held, however, that the brain is too "warm, wet and noisy" (as it's commonly summed up) to maintain coher-ence for meaningful amounts of time (Tegmark 2000). But others believe this is possible, and some have proposed concrete mechanisms for how it may occur (Beck and Eccles 1992; Hameroff and Penrose 2016).[34]

If brain states rather tend to *decohere*, or become entangled with the external environment, this would result in superposed macrostates involving both the brain and parts of the environment, all of which would then have to collapse together. The parts of the environment may include physical objects as well as

---

[33] Though not exactly the same, see Aaronson (2016).

[34] Note that Hameroff and Penrose's overarching Orch OR theory is not itself dualist (as it seems to *identify* consciousness with set of collapses of coherent states in the brain) but the mechanism it posits for sustaining coherence could still be co-opted by dualists.

other people. If consciousness influences the outcome of collapses of such superpositions, it would have an instant and direct influence over physical objects and other people of a kind we – at least on the face of it – don't seem to have.[35] It also leads to questions such as: what happens if different people involved in the same superposition (which could potentially be many) try to collapse it in different incompatible ways? Perhaps these and other issues can be sorted out, but this is somewhat unclear, as this possibility seems to have been little explored.

The second obstacle, however, is that even if one could identify superpositions whose outcome is decisive for behavior, the idea that consciousness influences these outcomes seems incompatible with quantum mechanics itself (Pereboom 1995; Montero and Papineau 2016). This is because even though quantum mechanics does not fix the outcome of a collapse, it does fix the *probability* of each outcome. And if consciousness gets involved in selecting the outcome, it must result in different probabilities than those assigned by quantum mechanics (i.e., higher for the selected outcome and lower for the others). Or, it might be suggested that conscious selection could in principle result in the same probabilities, but this would involve a coincidence akin to that posited by overdetermination dualism. It might also be suggested that quantum mechanics might not really fix the probabilities in cases where consciousness is involved, that is, deny that quantum mechanics is universal, but this is a radical claim from the scientific point of view, for which there is currently no evidence.

The idea that consciousness causes collapse without influencing its outcome[36] avoids this second obstacle (but not necessarily the first one, of identifying some superposition whose outcome is decisive for behavior and it would be possible for consciousness to collapse[37]). As mentioned, quantum mechanics tells us that superpositions will collapse (or at least appear to, depending on the interpretation) upon measurement, but it says nothing about what measurement consists in or why it leads to collapse. Physicists Eugene

---

[35] That is, according to standard quantum theory, we are able to instantly affect entangled objects arbitrarily far away via local measurement, but then we are only causing collapse without influencing the outcome. The idea discussed here is whether we can also influence the outcome of far-away collapses. Not only may this seem dubious in itself but, as Kelvin McQueen points out (in correspondence), it may also conflict with the no-signaling principle, according to which quantum information cannot be transferred faster than light.

[36] One might hold that consciousness both causes collapse and influences the outcome, but one can also hold one without the other.

[37] Such a state may be somewhat easier to find, however, if consciousness is not assumed to influence the outcome of collapse. Chalmers and McQueen, for example, assume that consciousness may collapse decoherent states, i.e., states involving both the brain and parts of the environment, but without influencing the outcome, and in that case the difficulties for this option mentioned above may not apply.

Wigner and John von Neumann both suggested[38] that measurement fundamentally consists in observation by a conscious being, but they did not develop the idea in detail. It resonated strongly, however, with authors associated with the 70s New Age movement, who went on to promote it to the public, and this may have contributed to giving it a reputation as unscientific (Chalmers and McQueen 2022, p. 4). David Chalmers and Kelvin McQueen (2022) have recently proposed a precise and scientifically grounded version of the idea (see also Stapp 1993).

According to this proposal, consciousness is superposition-resistant, meaning that it may go into superposition, but when it does, it will quickly collapse on its own. When a superposed physical system (such as a particle, or neuron) is measured, it becomes entangled with consciousness, and will therefore quickly collapse, too (on an earlier version of the proposal, consciousness can't be superposed at all; however, this turns out to imply that consciousness can't change, given what is known as the quantum Zeno effect (2022, p. 16) – hence they modify the proposal to allow for superposition of consciousness after all).

Chalmers and McQueen show that this view is empirically testable in principle, though currently not in practice. It should be noted that the view is compatible with both dualism and physicalism (on the physicalist version, it's the physical basis of consciousness that is superposition-resistant, rather than consciousness). Therefore, if it were to be empirically confirmed, it would not thereby confirm dualism as well. But it would still confirm the possibility of a causal role for non-physical consciousness compatible with physics, and thereby weaken (though not refute) the evidence for physical causal closure.

There is a question of whether the view that consciousness causes collapse without influencing the outcome offers the right kind of causal role for consciousness. Firstly, one might think that, if measurement is the only way by which the mental can affect the physical, our agency might seem to reduce to a kind of passive observation. But on Chalmers and McQueen's view, the kinds of conscious states that cause collapse need not always be measurements. On their view, consciousness primarily collapses physical states in the brain. Some of these states will be connected to perception and further entangled with measurement devices, and thus constitute measurements, but others may be connected to volition and behavior. Still, if agency consists in collapsing brain states, without influencing the outcome, its role will be limited to one of merely "rolling the dice" where the outcome is entirely random – which can also be regarded as fairly passive, or at least more so than we would like.

---

[38] Or alluded to, in von Neumann's case, but the view has still come to be associated with both him and Wigner (who was more explicit about the role of consciousness).

Another question is what it means for consciousness to exist in a superposed state. How could it possibly feel to have an experience superposed between, for example, blue (throughout the entire visual field) and orange? Or, would each state in the superposition be experienced in isolation, as though by parallel subjects? Many proponents of consciousness collapse theories, such as Wigner, have been explicitly motivated by how it doesn't seem to make sense for consciousness to be superposed (and so were Chalmers and McQueen, at least to some extent, before they discovered the conflict with the Zeno effect) – so if the more developed versions of the idea end up having to posit it after all, it loses some of its motivation and instead encounters a problem.

Summing up, the prospects for interactionism largely depend on how things turn out empirically, mainly in quantum physics and the physics of strong emergence. But even if it turns out in interactionism's favor, there are also philosophical challenges that must be resolved.

3 Subjective Idealism and Phenomenalism

Idealism is the view that reality is fundamentally mental. It can be divided into two kinds, which we may call subjective and objective, or alternatively, anti-realist and realist (Chalmers 2019a). Subjective or antirealist idealism takes the physical world to consist merely in appearances to, or perceptions within, the human or other broadly similar minds (such as the minds of complex animals or intelligent aliens). In other words, it takes the physical world to be dependent on the consciousness of external observers, or *observer-dependent* for short.[39] It is often thought that observer-dependence is incompatible with the physical world being fully real. Subjective idealism can therefore be understood as the view that reality is fundamentally mental *and* the physical does not really exist, but is rather a kind of illusion.

Objective or realist idealism, in contrast, can be understood as the view that reality is fundamentally mental, and the physical world is a structure of relations between mental experiences or subjects, rather than appearances to an observer, such that the physical world can (at least arguably) be regarded as fully real. This kind of idealism would be a version of dual-aspect monism, and will be explained and discussed in Section 4.[40]

---

[39] What is here called observer-dependence is often described as "mind-dependence," but according to objective or realist idealism, the physical world would be mind-dependent (in virtue of consisting of relations between minds or experiences) but not observer-dependent, and observer-dependence is more clearly in conflict with realism than mind-dependence without observer-dependence. Therefore, these two concepts should be separated.

[40] Note that there also many types of idealism, such as absolute idealism and German idealism, that make claims not only about the relationship between consciousness and the physical world, but also about a number of other issues such as the nature of knowledge, the structure and meaning of

In this section, we will also consider phenomenalism, a view that, like subjective idealism, links the physical world to appearances or perceptions of it, but in a different way: according to phenomenalism, the physical world consists in *potentials* for conscious perceptions, rather than in these perceptions themselves, as per subjective idealism.

3.1 Berkeleyan Idealism

The classic version of subjective idealism is due to George Berkeley. Berkeley argues that all that fundamentally exists are mental subjects and their *ideas*, which is his term for mental states in general, including perceptions, thoughts, and so on. His arguments for this do not start from the problem of explaining consciousness – that is, he does not argue that subjective idealism is the best explanation for how consciousness fits into reality. Rather, he argues that the idea of an observer-independent physical world is first of all *unproven*, that is, not supported by evidence, and secondly even *incoherent*, that is, that it doesn't really make sense in the first place.

According to Berkeley, our main evidence of the physical world is that we take ourselves to perceive it, but in fact, we only perceive our own ideas. It might be objected that we still perceive physical objects and properties *through* or *by means of* our ideas. But according to Berkeley, this would only be possible if our ideas somehow *resemble* physical objects or properties (e.g., we might perceive physical redness through perceiving phenomenal redness, but only insofar as phenomenal redness resembles physical redness), and it makes no sense that a mental idea and a physical object or property can resemble each other – since the physical and the mental would have a fundamentally different nature and things of fundamentally different natures cannot resemble each other.

Berkeley also argues that we can't really conceive of physical objects existing without being perceived. When we conceive of a tree, for example, existing unperceived, we are really conceiving of the perceptions we would have had of the tree *if* we perceived it. Thus, we are always implicitly conceiving of a perceiver along with any physical object, and the notion of an unperceived

---

history, and so on. These types of idealism fall outside the scope of this Element; however, the claims they do make about consciousness can often be interpreted as overlapping with either subjective idealism or dual-aspect monism. Also note that "idealism" may be used in a way that contrasts with realism (about the content of our perceptions, the external world, or similar) rather than with physicalism and other non-physicalist theories, for example, in the case of Immanuel Kant's transcendental idealism. Idealism in this sense is also outside our scope (Kant's view of consciousness could also be interpreted not as idealistic but rather as falling somewhere between mysterianism [see Conclusion] and dual-aspect panprotopsychism with unknown protophenomenal properties (see Section 4 and in particular footnote 52).

physical object is revealed as incoherent. Berkeley concludes that physical objects consist in nothing more than collections of perceptions, or as he sums it up: *esse est percipi* ("to be is to be perceived").

But if physical objects are nothing more than collections of perceptions, there arises a puzzle: how come our perceptions are so regularly and predictably organized? For example, if I perceive a tree outside my window, and then close my eyes, my perception of the tree will disappear, but when I open them again, the perception comes back. Usually, we would take this to be explained by the existence of a physical tree that causes our perceptions but still exists independently of them. If there are no observer-independent trees or other objects, the regularities between our perceptions would seem entirely inexplicable. It also implies that physical objects disappear entirely when not perceived by anyone. Both these consequences seem highly implausible.

Berkeley famously attempts to avoid both consequences by invoking God. Firstly, he takes God to be the source of our ideas and to ensure that they appear to us in a regular and predictable manner. Secondly, he claims that all ideas exist in God, meaning that physical objects will not disappear when not being perceived by us, because they will always be perceived by God.

Contemporary idealists, such as Foster (1982) and Robinson (1982), tend to follow Berkeley both in arguing that the idea of an observer-independent physical world is both unproven and hard to make sense of on reflection, and in regarding God as the source of our ideas and the explanation for the regularities we find within perception (though see Yetter-Chappell 2017 for an exception on the latter point).

3.2 Quantum Idealism

One might think subjective idealism could also be supported in an entirely different way than Berkeley's, namely by appeal to quantum mechanics. As discussed in Section 2, the quantum wave function describes objects as superposed between different possible states, which appear to collapse into determinate states upon measurement, and measurement can be interpreted as involving conscious observation or perception. This may be taken to suggest that reality comes into being only when perceived, in accordance with Berkeley's *esse est percipi* slogan – as alluded to, for example, by physicist Wheeler (1983).[41]

However, this doesn't quite follow. First, as also discussed, there are many interpretations of quantum mechanics where collapse is caused by something

---

[41] Wheeler cites Berkeley's slogan with some degree of approval, but he makes several qualifications and also denies that perception requires consciousness, so he clearly doesn't endorse subjective idealism.

other than conscious observation or where there is no collapse at all. Second, even on the interpretation where consciousness causes collapse, reality exists prior to interaction with consciousness in a superposed state, and interaction with consciousness only brings it into a different, determinate (i.e., unsuperposed) state (thereby changing rather than creating it). Third, the collapse interpretation takes consciousness to *cause* the transition from superposed to determinate reality, and since causes and effects are distinct, this does not imply that determinate reality is *identical* with conscious states, as per subjective idealism – otherwise, the interpretation would not be compatible with dualism (as Chalmers and McQueen maintain it is).

In addition to the interpretation where consciousness causes collapse, an interpretation known a QBism (Fuchs, Mermin, and Schack 2014) has also been taken as suggestive of subjective idealism (e.g., Brown 2019). According to QBism, the probabilities that can be derived from the wave function should be interpreted as expressing "the beliefs of the agent who makes [predictions based on them], and refer to that same agent's expectations for her subsequent experiences" (Fuchs et al. 2014, p. 749). That is, the probabilities are purely *subjective* probabilities, or expressions of our own judgments about how likely something is to happen, as opposed to objective frequencies or propensities in the external world. Collapse should be interpreted as consisting of agents updating (i.e., changing, in view of newly acquired evidence) their subjective probabilities (hence the name QBism, which originally stood for Quantum Bayesianism, Bayesianism being a theory of how subjective probabilities should be updated). Furthermore, the probabilities, as QBism interprets them, concern our own experiences rather than physical events. If quantum mechanics thus only describes our own beliefs and experiences, that could be taken to suggest that reality consists in nothing more than such mental phenomena.

But QBism can also be understood in other ways, for example, as a form of instrumentalism: a view according to which quantum mechanics is merely a tool for making predictions, rather than a description of reality, and thus completely neutral on the nature of reality (similarly to the Copenhagen interpretation, which has also been taken to imply subjective idealism, though it's more standardly regarded as a form of instrumentalism [see Healey 2022 for discussion of this and other ways of understanding of QBism and similar interpretations]). QBism's main proponents also deny that it should be understood as any kind of idealism (Fuchs 2015) (though they are less clear about exactly how it should be classified instead). If QBism is nevertheless understood as a form of subjective idealism, it would face essentially the same problem as Berkeleyan idealism of explaining why our experiences are so regularly and predictably organized (i.e., why can our experiences be predicted by quantum mechanics, if there is no underlying quantum reality that causes them, or at least not one like quantum mechanics seems to describe?).

3.3 Subjective Idealism and the Arguments for and against Physicalism

As mentioned, subjective idealism has not mainly been defended as a solution to the problem of consciousness, but how does it stand up when considered as one? In response to the unity arguments against physicalism, subjective idealism may posit subjects understood as mental substances in addition to experiences (or ideas). It can therefore accommodate the unity arguments as well as substance dualism can, but it also seems compatible with the deflationary view.

With respect to the arguments for physicalism, subjective idealism offers fairly straightforward responses to the arguments from physical causal closure and the argument from previous explanatory successes. Since subjective idealism regards physical objects as mere collections of perceptions, the evidence for physical causal closure can be interpreted not as evidence of physical events having sufficient physical causes, but rather as evidence for particular regularities holding between various kinds of perceptions or experiences, and thereby as entirely compatible with subjective idealism. The previous explanatory successes of science can also be interpreted as revealing regularities between perceptions of higher-level complex phenomena (life, diseases, and so on) and perceptions of lower-level mechanisms or realizers (DNA, germs, and so on, or the traces of them we perceive in microscopes or through other measurements), rather than as revealing that the higher-level phenomena are physically constituted.

The response to the argument from mind–brain correlations is slightly more complicated. Subjective idealism can't account for correlations between conscious states and brain states in the same way it accounts for correlations between perceptions and objects perceived, that is, by identifying the objects with the perceptions. This is because conscious states are not perceptions of the brain states they correlate with (e.g., an experience of red may be correlated with some activity in the visual cortex of a brain, but it's not a perception of this brain activity; rather, it would be part of the perception of a red object outside the brain such as an apple or tomato). Instead, brain states must be regarded as perceptions of one subject (a person observing someone else's brain) and the conscious states as the perceptions or other conscious states of another subject (the person whose brain is being observed). This underscores how subjective idealism needs to posit correlations not only between different perceptions of the same subject (e.g., my perception of a tree before I close my eyes and my next perception after I reopen them) but also between the perceptions of different subjects (unless subjective idealism is combined with solipsism, which it need not be). Mind–brain correlations would be a correlation of the second kind. This explanation of mind–brain correlations is just as simple as physicalism's explanation in the sense that both theories posit just one fundamental kind of properties (mental only, given subjective idealism, and physical only, given physicalism).

However, subjective idealism is left with the major question of why the regularities between our perceptions (both within and between subjects) hold. Leaving them unexplained suggests they are simply coincidental, which seems extremely implausible, and explaining them in terms of God leads to a number of objections. For example, that God directly produces and organizes our perceptions can be regarded as a complicated hypothesis that renders subjective idealism far less simple than physicalism overall. In addition, the explanation must arguably be supported by independent arguments for the existence of God (such as the cosmological argument, the ontological argument, or other classic arguments for theism), which many find unconvincing – though even believers might find subjective idealism an implausible account of how God has organized creation.

One alternative possibility is to take the regularities to be explained by fundamental mental laws, which would arguably be no more inexplicable than the fundamental physical laws (Yetter-Chappell 2017). But mental laws coordinating perceptions would have to be highly complicated compared to the physical laws. Among other reasons, this would be because, if human-type experiences are fundamental, there would be a vastly higher number of fundamental entities than those posited by physics (that is, physics currently posits about seventeen fundamental particles, but the types of human experience are countless) and this would require a vastly more complicated set of laws to govern them.

3.4 Phenomenalism

The classic version of phenomenalism is due to John Stuart Mill.[42] According to this view, physical objects are understood as potentials for, or dispositions to produce, perceptions – or as Mill puts it: "permanent possibilities of sensation" – rather than collections of perceptions themselves. For example, an apple should be understood as a potential to produce experiences of redness, sweetness, and so on, in most human perceivers. A potential or disposition can exist

---

[42] Phenomenalism is also associated with logical positivism (of the 1920s Vienna Circle), but then primarily understood as a theory of linguistic or theoretical meaning, rather than as a theory of fundamental reality. In addition, phenomenalism can refer to a view exactly like subjective idealism, according to which physical objects are nothing but collections of perceptions (rather than potentials for perceptions), except that it posits no explanation for the regularities between these perceptions in terms of either God or anything else. This kind of phenomenalism will be set aside in this subsection since it has effectively been discussed in the previous one. For a detailed introduction to various kinds of phenomenalism, see Hirst (2006).

unactualized or unmanifested (i.e., it could be true that a perception *would* have been produced if an observer had been present, even if no perception was in fact produced because no observer was present). The stable existence of these potentials implies that physical objects will not disappear when unperceived, and it can also explain why physical objects appear to us in a regular way when they are perceived – thus solving the two main problems of subjective idealism.

Like phenomenalism, our ordinary view of the physical world also takes physical objects to have potentials to cause perceptions. But on the ordinary view, physical objects will also, and primarily, have potentials to cause effects on other physical objects (i.e., such as movement, heat, and so on, rather than just perceptions), and some physical objects won't have the potential to directly cause perceptions at all (e.g., particles invisible to the naked eye). According to phenomenalism, at least the classic version, physical objects are potentials to produce perceptions and nothing else. Another difference is that, on the ordinary view, potentials or dispositions are explained by or grounded in underlying physical structures or qualities (e.g., the disposition of a magnet to attract metal is explained in terms of its underlying configuration of electrons). According to phenomenalism, potentials to produce experience are basic, that is, not grounded in any underlying structure or properties.

One typical objection to phenomenalism is that potentials can't be brute, that is, exist ungrounded or without any further basis (such as an underlying physical structure). However, in recent years, a number of philosophers who don't endorse phenomenalism have argued that fundamental physical properties are in fact nothing more than brute dispositions or potentials (Shoemaker 1980; Mumford 2004) – this view is known as dispositionalism and will be discussed further in Section 4.

Another objection is that it's implausible for the fundamental potentials of physical objects to be directed towards producing perceptions alone. Not only does this seem quite anthropocentric (i.e., to offer humans an unreasonably central place in nature), it also goes against physics, which – like the ordinary view just discussed – describes physical objects as having all sorts of other dispositions as well. Going against physics may be regarded as a problem in itself, but it may also require positing a set of laws governing the potentials vastly more complicated than the laws of physics (for reasons analogous to why subjective idealism would require complicated laws, such as there being far more types of potentials than types of fundamental physical entities).

Pelczar (2023) has recently given an elaborate defense of phenomenalism against these and other objections, according to which potentials for experience can also have potentials to affect other potentials (rather than only affecting consciousness directly), making them able to mirror the structure of the physical world as described by physics. One problem with this response, however, is that it blurs the distinction between phenomenalism and dualism (if consciousness is regarded as distinct from the potentials), as the world of potentials will begin to look quite indistinguishable from the physical world as the aforementioned dispositionalists see it. That is, physical objects will look like potentials for physical effects primarily, with some mental or perceptual effects in addition, rather than potentials for perceptions primarily.

3.5 Phenomenalism and the Arguments for and against Physicalism

Like substance dualism and subjective idealism, phenomenalism may posit subjects understood as mental substances in addition to perceptions, and is therefore also compatible with the unity arguments, but it can also be combined with the deflationary view of subjects.

In its responses to the arguments for physicalism, phenomenalism has more in common with dualism than subjective idealism. This is because it could, as already hinted at, be considered a kind of dualism, since it posits fundamental consciousness on the one hand, and fundamental potentials for perceptions that are not themselves mental on the other.

As an explanation of mind–brain correlations, this is no more parsimonious than dualism. It also leads to a conflict with physical causal closure basically identical to that of dualism (Pelczar 2019, pp. 18–19).[43] Given phenomenalism, the evidence for physical causal closure can be interpreted as evidence that changes in potentials are fully caused by other potentials, rather than by perceptions or other mental phenomena. It follows that the mental is affected by physical potentials, but either does not affect them in return (i.e., is epiphenomenal) or affects them in an overdetermining way. Phenomenalism thereby faces the same choice as dualism between epiphenomenalism, overdetermination and denying physical causal closure, and this choice seems as difficult given phenomenalism as given dualism. Therefore, phenomenalism does not clearly offer any unique advantages as a theory of consciousness.

4 Dual-Aspect Monism (or Panpsychism and Panprotopsychism)

Dual-aspect monism claims that reality consists of one fundamental kind of stuff, but that this stuff has two different aspects throughout, a physical aspect

---

[43] Pelczar (2019) points to this as a problem, but argues that phenomenalism, unlike dualism, still offers phenomenal properties non-causal relevance to the physical world in virtue of their close connection to physical potentials – but he later changed his mind and no longer regards this as real advantage (expressed in correspondence).

and a mental or protomental aspect – where the protomental is understood roughly as non-physical precursors to the fully mental.

Since everything has both aspects, dual-aspect monism implies *panpsychism*, the view that consciousness is everywhere (*pan* is Greek for "everything" and *psyche* for "mind" or "consciousness"), or alternatively, *panprotopsychism*, that protoconsciousness is everywhere (*proto* is Greek for "first" or "preceding"). This is to say that even non-living entities (that also, unlike, e.g., robots or AI, have no functional overlap with us), such as fundamental particles, have some fundamental form of consciousness or protoconsciousness. Complex consciousness, such as human and animal consciousness, is in turn taken to result from fundamental consciousness or protoconsciousness (or the particles possessing it) being put together in the right way.

Furthermore, the reason why everything (including particles) has both a physical and a (proto)mental aspect, according to dual-aspect monism, is that (proto)consciousness is the *intrinsic* nature of physical properties, which physics reveals as purely *structural* or *relational*. That is, according to dual-aspect monism, when we look at what physics tells us about reality, we see that it only tells us – to put it roughly – how reality is from the *outside*, or about the relations between things (such as causal relations and spatiotemporal relations).

But every outside needs an *inside*, or relations need relata (i.e., things that stand in the relations) with *intrinsic* properties (i.e., properties that characterize them as they are *in themselves*, independently of their relations).[44] And it turns out we do know the inside, or intrinsic properties, of one physical thing, namely ourselves: our own consciousness, or its phenomenal qualities, seem intrinsic. Phenomenal consciousness or protoconsciousness could therefore be the inside, or intrinsic properties, of everything physical.

Thus, dual-aspect monism can be more precisely defined as the view that (1) phenomenal properties are not physical, but rather either fundamental or constituted by protophenomenal properties, and (2) physical properties are relations between, or structures of, phenomenal or protophenomenal properties (from which it follows that everything physical is also mental or protomental).

Dual-aspect monism is also widely known as *Russellian monism*, after Bertrand Russell, who defended many of its central claims (1927, 1948), though it's unclear whether he fully endorsed it.[45] Other historical proponents

---

[44] These intrinsic properties are often referred to as *quiddities*.

[45] Russell clearly endorsed a view he called *neutral monism*, which was first proposed by Ernst Mach and William James. This view is somewhat difficult to interpret and categorize, but seems to incorporate elements from other views (such as subjective idealism, phenomenalism or panprotopsychism) combined with some unique additional features (see Stubenberg 2018 for a detailed overview of neutral monism in this sense and its various interpretations). But neutral monism can also be understood in a different sense that overlaps more or less exactly with dual-aspect

(of at least parts of the view) include, for example, G. W. Leibniz and Arthur Schopenhauer.[46] In the twentieth century, it was kept alive by philosophers such as Maxwell (1979), Sprigge (1983), Lockwood (1989), and to some extent Russell's collaborator Whitehead (1929) (by whom Russell's version may have been inspired) and his follower Hartshorne (1937), but it was not widely recognized as a distinct and interesting alternative to other non-physicalist theories. In the last few decades, however, it has become more widely recognized as such based on defenses by philosophers such as Chalmers (1995, 1996, 2003, 2013, 2016), Seager (1995, 2010), Stoljar (2001), Strawson (2006b, 2016), and Goff (2017).

Here, the view will be referred to mainly as dual-aspect (rather than Russellian) monism, partly because it's not uniquely associated with Russell, but mainly because this term is more directly descriptive. *Aspects* can be understood roughly as properties that appear or not depending on the point of view – the physical aspect being those properties that appear from the outside, third-person, or scientific point of view, whereas the mental or protomental being those properties that appear from the inside, first-person or introspective point of view. *Monism* is the view that there is one kind of stuff (or kind of things) – that the physical and (proto)mental are both aspects of.[47]

Monism is thus the opposite of substance dualism, and it should be noted that physicalism, subjective idealism and property dualism are also monist views. However, physicalism differs from dual-aspect monism in taking the one stuff

---

panprotopsychism, since protophenomenal properties are *neutral* in the sense of neither physical nor mental. Whether Russell fully endorsed neutral monism is this latter sense is not clear, but in his 1927 and 1948 he clearly suggests something very close. Also note that neutral monism in the former (Machian or Jamesian) sense will not be discussed further because of the interpretive difficulties, which make it hard to pinpoint any unique advantages it may have as a theory of consciousness.

[46] These philosophers are often classified as idealists, but their idealism is closer to the objective than the subjective kind (as distinguished in Section 3), or *pure* dual-aspect monism, to be discussed in Section 4.3. See also Skrbina (2005) for an overview of numerous other historical proponents of panpsychism (though not always the dual-aspect version).

[47] Dual-aspect monism should also be distinguished from the view held by Baruch Spinoza, which is often described as dual-aspect monism as well. Spinoza's endorses "thing monism," according to which reality consists in a single substance understood as one unified thing. Dual-aspect monism (as defined here) only implies "stuff monism" or "kind monism," according to which there may exist a number of different things, but only one fundamental *kind* of things, or kind of stuff they are all made of (though there can also be thing-monistic versions of the view, such as cosmopsychism, to be discussed later). Another difference is that while Spinoza also claims reality has two aspects (or *attributes*), thought and extension, it's not clear whether he intends "thought" to include phenomenal consciousness (Spinoza may thereby differ from Descartes, who also characterizes mental substances in terms of thinking, but explicitly (*Meditations*, II) takes thinking to include, e.g., imagining and sensing, which can be interpreted to involve phenomenal consciousness). It's also unclear whether Spinoza regards extension as purely structural.

or substance to have only physical properties throughout (and taking mental properties to be constituted by physical properties) and subjective idealism in taking it to only have mental properties throughout and taking physical properties to be observer-dependent and in that sense not fully real. Property dualism differs mainly in taking physical and mental properties to be causally related rather than as relations/relata or "inside/outside," or as sharply distinct rather than two complementary aspects (in addition, it typically takes only *some*, rather than all, things to have mental properties in addition to their physical ones).

4.1 The Background for Dual-Aspect Monism

According to dual-aspect monism, physics leaves a gap in its description of reality, not just because it appears to leave out consciousness (by leaving an epistemic gap to it), but because it only tells us about the *structure* of reality, or equivalently, about the *relations* between things (as structures can be understood as sets of relations). These relations may include spatiotemporal relations (i.e., distances, temporal order, and so on), causal relations (i.e., which things affect each other and how), and mathematical and logical relations. Or, as it's also often put, physics only tells us about *dispositions*, or what things would *do* in given circumstances.[48]

For example, physics tells us that fundamental particles have properties such as mass and charge. But charge is just to attract particles with the opposite charge and repel particles with the same charge. And mass is just to resist acceleration, attract other things gravitationally, and so on. In other words, mass and charge are just ways of behaving or relating to other things. Or consider extension, which Descartes regarded as the essential property of the physical. As was pointed out by Leibniz, to be extended is just to occupy an area, and to occupy an area is simply to resist or prevent other things from entering, and therefore a mere behavior as well (Blackburn 1990).

More generally, it can also be observed how fundamental physics is formulated purely in terms of mathematics (such as Schrödinger's equation or Newton's equations), and mathematics can be regarded as a language that describes relations only – for example, all we know about the number 2 is

---

[48] Dispositions could be understood as pure relations between the behavior disposed towards and the circumstances or stimuli that trigger it (roughly on the format "will do X given circumstance Y"). If so, the claim that physics only describes dispositions is compatible with the claim that physics only describes relations – though not equivalent, since the latter claim allows that some relations may not be purely dispositional, such as spatiotemporal relations. A different understanding of dispositions, and an objection to dual-aspect monism on this basis, will be discussed in Section 4.4.2.

how it relates to other numbers and mathematical objects (e.g., that it's larger than 1, smaller then 3, half of 4, and so on) (see, e.g., Shapiro 1997; Gowers 2002). It follows that physics also describes relations only.

Dual-aspect monism then claims that there must be something that stands in these relations, or performs the behavior, something that also has intrinsic or categorical properties. Intrinsic properties are here understood as properties that characterize things as they are in themselves, or independently of their relations to other things, as well as to themselves and to or between their own parts (if any),[49] and categorical properties are properties that are not merely dispositional, or that characterize how things *are* as opposed to merely what they *do*.[50]

In other words, the structure described by physics must be realized or implemented by something that is itself not purely structural – roughly in the same way a piece of software (which can be understood as a pure set of logical relations) cannot exist, at least not concretely and physically, unless there is some hardware that implements it (and the "hardware" doesn't just consist in further software, as in a virtual machine). Or, as physicist Stephen Hawking has put it, in a passage much cited by dual-aspect monists[51]: "even if there is only one possible unified theory, it is just a set of rules and equations. What is it that breathes fire into the equations and makes a universe for them to describe?" (Hawking 1988, p. 174).

If physics doesn't tell us about this "fire" or "hardware," understood as the intrinsic realizers of the mathematical structure described by physics, it's hard to see what it could be. Some have concluded that the intrinsic properties of the physical must therefore be forever unknowable (Langton 1998; Lewis 2009).[52] Dual-aspect monists have pointed out, however, that consciousness, or its phenomenal qualities, seem intrinsic: we know something about how they are *in themselves*, beyond their relations to anything else (such as their causes and effects), namely *what they are like* or their qualities. Indeed, it's precisely for this reason that phenomenal consciousness seems to go beyond mere functioning: a function is roughly equal to a disposition or set of relations (between causes and effects, or inputs and outputs), but phenomenal consciousness involves qualities that seem to go beyond this.

This suggests the possibility that consciousness is what realizes physical structure, or that the relations described by physics are relations between

---

[49] See Pereboom (2015) for a discussion of this versus other notions of the intrinsic.

[50] Intrinsic and categorical properties can be regarded as roughly equivalent (or the latter as a subspecies of the former), in the same way their counterparts of relational and dispositional properties can (see footnote 48).

[51] Hawking himself did not endorse dual-aspect monism in other respects.

[52] Langton also interprets Immanuel Kant's claim that things in themselves are unknowable to this effect.

phenomenal experiences. Most of these experiences would not be experiences of humans, animals or other complex entities or systems, but rather of simple entities such as particles. These experiences can be assumed to be extremely simple, or as simple compared to ours as their physical structure is.

Alternatively, one might regard the realizers as merely protoconscious. Protophenomenal properties are, to define them more precisely, intrinsic properties that are neither physical nor phenomenal, but are able to constitute (or, alternatively, causally produce) phenomenal properties when put together in the right way.

Dual-aspect panpsychism thereby turns physicalism on its head, by taking the physical to be realized by the mental, or at least protomental, or – in terms of the computationalist version of physicalism – by regarding the physical as software and consciousness as the hardware, rather than the other way around.[53]

4.2 Arguments for Dual-Aspect Monism

4.2.1 The Argument from the Intrinsic Nature of the Physical

So far, we have seen that dual-aspect monists make the following claims:

1. Physical properties are all structural (or relational, dispositional).
2. Structural properties have realizers with intrinsic (or non-relational categorical) properties.
3. Phenomenal or protophenomenal properties are intrinsic.

This suggests, but doesn't establish, that (proto)consciousness is the intrinsic realizer of physical structure, because there could be other kinds of intrinsic properties that can play this role, too. For example, one might think there are other intrinsic properties that are unknown to us, or that we can know or imagine other intrinsic properties besides consciousness.

The argument could be completed by adding two further claims. Firstly, that consciousness is the only intrinsic property we know, and that all other purported options (such as shape or physical colors) turn out to be relational on examination (e.g., shape is reducible to spatial relations, and physical colors are mere dispositions to cause phenomenal colors in observers, or similar). It is also arguably the only intrinsic property we can imagine. Panprotopsychists might add that protoconsciousness could be known or imagined on the basis of consciousness.

This still leaves the possibility of positing intrinsic properties that are completely unknowable and unimaginable. But why posit unknown properties when there are known ones, i.e., consciousness or protoconsciousness, able to do the

---

[53] For a more elaborate, accessible introduction to the background for dual-aspect monism, see Mørch (2021) or Goff (2019).

job? In other areas of inquiry, we usually posit unknown properties in our theories only when there are no suitable known ones (e.g., in the case of dark matter), and arguably, the same standard should be applied in this case.

To complete the argument, then, it can be added that:

4. Phenomenal or protophenomenal properties are the only intrinsic properties we know.
5. We should not posit unknown properties if there are known alternatives.

This gives the conclusion:

6. Physical properties have realizers with (proto)phenomenal properties.

4.2.2 The "Solving Two Problems at Once" Argument (or Dual-Aspect Monism and the Arguments for Physicalism)

The argument discussed in the previous subsection is not based on the problem of explaining consciousness, but only on the problem of explaining the intrinsic nature of the physical. Dual-aspect monism could be defended based on this kind of argument alone (Seager 2006; Adams 2007). But it is another argument, that *is* based on the problem of explaining consciousness, that is mainly responsible for the recent resurgence of interest in the view.

According to this argument, positing consciousness or protoconsciousness as the intrinsic nature of the physical also offers the best explanation of how consciousness fits into the physical world, because it avoids the main problems of both physicalism and dualism at once (Alter and Nagasawa 2012; Chalmers 2013). The main problem of physicalism is the epistemic gap. Since dual-aspect monism regards consciousness as non-physical, it is compatible with the epistemic gap – just like dualism. The main problem of dualism, on the other hand, is the argument from physical causal closure. In response to this, dual-aspect monism claims that, as the realizers of physical structure, consciousness gets an explanatory role compatible with physical causal closure (Stoljar 2001; Chalmers 2003, 2013; Alter and Nagasawa 2012).

The This latter response requires some elaboration. The response starts from distinguishing two different versions of the principle of physical causal closure, a narrow and a broad version (Stoljar 2001; Chalmers 2013). The narrow version claims that every physical effect has a *purely* physical cause, or cause with only physical (or physically constituted) properties. But according to dual-aspect monism, a purely physical cause would be a purely structural entity, and structures arguably cannot really exist without being realized by something with intrinsic properties – in the same way software cannot really exist without hardware. If purely physical causes cannot even exist, they would not be sufficient to cause anything, so the narrow principle must be false.

The broad version claims every physical effect has a sufficient cause whose *structural* properties are all physical. Or put another way, that the only causal structure needed to explain physical effects is physical causal structure, where physical causal structure could be understood as causal relations that fall under physical laws. According to dual-aspect monism, the broad principle is what the scientific evidence for physical causal closure really supports, since this evidence mainly consists in the fact that all causal relations required to explain physical events examined so far fall under physical laws.

But the broad principle is compatible with dual-aspect monism, because it says nothing about whether the causal relations or structure also have intrinsic realizers, such as phenomenal or protophenomenal realizers. And if structure requires intrinsic realizers in order to exist, phenomenal or protophenomenal realizers would not be epiphenomenal or overdetermining, but rather have an essential explanatory role. This explanatory role may be described as causal, since by enabling the existence of physical causes (proto)consciousness would clearly be relevant to causation, but since this relevance would be different than that of physical properties, the role could also be described as constitutive or explanatory in a broader sense. Either way, consciousness will play a significant, non-redundant role as the realizer of physical processes, including our own physical behavior.

The broad version of the principle still rules out interactionist dualism, because interactionist dualism claims that some physical events (i.e., our behavior) require explanation in term of causal relations that do not fall under physical laws, but rather under fundamental psychophysical laws. In other words, interactionist dualism posits additional causal structure that is not physical, and which, unlike the structure posited by epiphenomenalist or overdetermination dualism, would be required to explain some physical events (i.e., behavior). The response therefore supports dual-aspect monism only, as opposed to non-physicalism more generally.

Dual-aspect monism can also respond to the other main arguments for physicalism, though in less original ways. The response to the argument from mind–brain correlations is roughly the same as that of subjective idealism, namely that as a monistic theory dual-aspect monism is as parsimonious as physicalism.[54] Second, its response to the argument from previous explanatory successes is mainly the same as that of dualism, namely that previously

---

[54] Or at least *almost* as parsimonious, if physical relations are regarded as fundamental as per the impure version of the view – this will be discussed in Section 4.3.

explained phenomena are functional or structural, whereas consciousness is not, and therefore one cannot generalize from the former to the latter.

In addition to the problems of physicalism and dualism, dual-aspect monism also avoids the problems of subjective idealism, since in taking the physical world as observer-independent and as having the exact structure described by physics, it can be regarded as a form of realism about the physical world – though this is more rarely emphasized (given the low popularity of subjective idealism compared to dualism and physicalism).[55]

4.2.3 The Argument from Non-emergence

In addition to the argument from the intrinsic nature of the physical and the argument from "solving two problems at once," there are two additional arguments especially worth noting.[56]

The first is the argument from non-emergence. This argument claims that consciousness cannot emerge from anything purely physical, or from putting together physical entities, such as particles, in the right way. But our own consciousness seems to emerge from particles in the brain. It follows that these particles cannot be purely physical but must rather have been fundamentally conscious or protoconscious all along. A stronger version of the argument claims that consciousness cannot emerge from anything *non-conscious*, or from putting together non-conscious entities in the right way. It follows that fundamental particles must be conscious, rather than merely protoconscious.

The weak version of the argument is discussed but ultimately rejected by Nagel (1979), even though he cannot say exactly how it goes wrong, because he regards the pan(proto)psychist conclusion as too implausible (he also briefly invokes a version of the combination problem, to be discussed below).[57] The strong version of the argument is both defended and endorsed by Strawson (2006b).

Both Nagel and Strawson claim that consciousness cannot be constituted by the physical, in view of the epistemic gap or closely related considerations. If it emerges from the physical, it must therefore be by something akin to causal production, or in accordance with a dualist psychophysical law.[58] Against this,

---

[55] Phenomenalism is usually ignored as well, but dual-aspect monism avoids both its problem of ungrounded dispositions (by grounding them in the (proto)mental) and the problems it shares with dualism.

[56] Other important arguments, that are nevertheless less central to the current debate and so will be skipped here, include the argument from continuity (James 1890, pp. 146–150; Goff 2014) and the argument from causation (Mørch 2018, 2019a) – though the latter will be briefly discussed as a possible response to the objection from pure dispositionalism in Section 4.4.2.

[57] Much later (2012), Nagel endorses a kind of panpsychism after all, but based on different arguments (which do not clearly fit the general picture of dual-aspect monism so will be set aside here).

[58] Nagel is explicit about this point; Strawson less so but can interpreted as implicitly endorsing it.

they both invoke considerations similar to those figuring in the interaction problem (Section 2.2), according to which such causal relations between the mental and the physical would be unintelligible and hence impossible. Nagel similarly claims that it's unintelligible how any physical process can necessitate consciousness (and that causation must involve necessitation, rather than effects merely "following" causes, as per the Humean view that, as noted, can also be invoked against the interaction problem). Strawson claims, also similarly, that the emergence of consciousness from the physical would be an instance of *brute* emergence, understood as emergence that is unintelligible in principle (or "unintelligible even to God," as he puts it), because there is simply nothing about the physical – if understood as completely devoid of consciousness – in virtue of which consciousness could emerge.

Note that this argument supports panpsychism (given the strong version) or panprotopsychism (given the weak version) understood simply as the view that fundamental physical entities are conscious or protoconscious, but not necessarily the dual-aspect versions, according to which fundamental physical entities are conscious or protoconscious specifically *because* this is the intrinsic nature of their physical structure.[59] But the argument is still compatible with dual-aspect monism (and this is also the version of panpsychism Strawson endorses).

4.2.4 The Argument from the Integrated Information Theory

Another argument for panpsychism (in this case, panprotopsychism is not included) derives from the Integrated Information Theory (IIT), a neuroscientific theory of consciousness developed by Giulio Tononi (later joined by Christof Koch and others) (Tononi 2008; Tononi, Albantakis, and Oizumi 2014).

The central claim of the theory is that consciousness is correlated with *maximal integrated information*, or maximal Φ ("*phi*") for short, which is a structural property with a precise mathematical definition. In short, everything that has maximal integrated information is conscious, and the higher the integrated information the higher the level of consciousness.

---

[59] That is, pan(proto)psychists could in principle take (proto)mental and physical properties to be related in other ways. For example, one might endorse a dualist version of panpsychism, according to which the fundamental psychophysical laws dictate that all physical things have mental properties or are connected to mental substances, or a physicalist version, according to which consciousness is constituted by a ubiquitous physical property (such as energy, or integrated information, as will be discussed in the next subsection). Non-dual-aspect versions of pan(proto)psychism cannot be supported by the arguments from the intrinsic nature of the physical or "solving two problems at once," and have no clear advantages compared to non-pan (proto)psychist versions of dualism or physicalism, so there is little reason to endorse them.

Very roughly,[60] information (as IIT defines it, which is quite different from how it is otherwise defined) is as a measure of the extent to which a system causally constrains its own past or future state (i.e., how much can you tell about the next and previous state of the system by looking only at the system itself, ignoring external influences?), and *integration* is as a measure of the extent to which this information depends on the causal interconnections between the system's parts (i.e., by cutting the system in two, thus severing the connections between the two parts, how much information in the previous sense is lost?). Finally, a system has *maximal* integrated information or Φ if it has more integrated information than any overlapping system, that is, any of its own parts or any larger system it is itself a part of.

The brain contains very high levels of Φ, especially in those areas that (according to IIT's proponents) appear necessary for consciousness. But small amounts of Φ can also be found at the level of fundamental physics, for example, in protons and neutrons (Koch 2012). It follows that these particles have a small amount of consciousness – unless they are part of a larger system with even higher Φ (such as a brain, cell, or molecule) which would then be conscious instead. IIT thereby implies panpsychism, or at least something quite close.[61] As with the argument from non-emergence, this panpsychism need not be of the dual-aspect sort, but it can be.[62]

Still, IIT is a controversial theory, both in view of the empirical (i.e., experimental and observational) evidence and for various theoretical reasons (see, e.g., Aaronson 2014; Bayne 2018a). An argument for panpsychism based on it would therefore be hostage to the empirical evidence turning out in its favor, and perhaps some further clarification and defense of its theoretical foundations.

4.3 Versions of Dual-Aspect Monism

Dual-aspect monism comes in different versions. We have already distinguished the panpsychist from the panprotopsychist version. Panprotopsychism can be further subdivided into different types based on their specific accounts of the

---

[60] For a more elaborate non-technical introduction to IIT, see Mørch (2017b).

[61] Note that Tononi and Koch (2015) deny that IIT leads to panpsychism, but they understand panpsychism as the view that all thinkable things (including tables, chairs, and rocks) are conscious in the sense of having *unified* consciousness (or in other words, as implying universal combination as discussed in Section 4.4.1). Integrated Information Theory clearly implies panpsychism in the more restrictive sense that all things are either (1) conscious, (2) made of conscious parts, such as conscious particles, or (3) itself part of a larger conscious whole – or at least something quite close. The main reason why it is only close is that whereas some fundamental particles, such as quarks, are never found in isolation and will therefore always be part of systems with some Φ and therefore some consciousness, other particles, such as photons, can be found in isolation and might therefore have no Φ and no consciousness. However, IIT as it stands is not really defined to apply to fundamental physics and it might therefore be possible to interpret it implying that even isolated particles have some Φ.

[62] At least with certain modifications – see Mørch (2019b, 2019c) for some obstacles to combining IIT with dual-aspect panpsychism as IIT currently stands and ways to modify IIT to enable it after all.

nature of protophenomenal properties. Some panprotopsychists don't specify the nature of protophenomenal properties at all: they regard them as entirely unknown. But if we know nothing about what the supposedly protophenomenal properties are like, how can we know they are really able to explain consciousness? This kind of panprotopsychism also can't be supported by the claim (part of the argument from the intrinsic nature of the physical) that we shouldn't posit unknown properties when known alternatives exist, since phenomenal properties would be a known alternative.

Others claim that protophenomenal properties should be conceived as unexperienced qualities (Coleman 2012) – this view is known as panqualityism. These unexperienced qualities are roughly equal to how we intuitively think of physical qualities, such as colors, when nobody is perceiving them, or as phenomenal qualities with only a qualitative (or "what it's like") but no subjective (or "for the subject") component (as distinguished in Section 1.1).

Panqualityism faces objections such as that it's hard to conceive of unexperienced qualities (as Berkeley would say, all we can conceive of is what they would be like *if* experienced), or that it's hard to see how to get experienced qualities from putting together unexperienced qualities in the right way. Positing protophenomenal properties may therefore seem problematic, whether known or unknown. But panprotopsychism may still have advantages over panpsychism in how it is able to respond to certain objections to dual-aspect monism – this will be discussed below.

Other distinctions can be explained mainly in terms of panpsychism, since analogous distinctions will hold for panprotopsychism (unless otherwise mentioned). First, there is a distinction between *pure* and *impure* panpsychism (Strawson 2006a; Chalmers 2019a). Pure panpsychism claims that physical relations are wholly constituted by their phenomenal relata. This is to say that reality is fundamentally mental and mental only. Pure panpsychism would thereby count as a version of idealism (i.e., the view that everything is fundamentally mental), but of the objective or realist as opposed to subjective or antirealist kind (see Section 3), since given pure panpsychism the physical world would consist in relations between mental relata with the same structure as described by physics, rather than appearances to observers which would have a different structure than that described by physics, as follows from subjective or antirealist idealism (pure panprotopsychism differs from subjective idealism in addition, of course, by positing non-mental protophenomenal properties).

Pure panpsychism is based on the observation that at least some relations seem to follow from their relata alone. For example, the relation of "being similar," that holds between red and orange, seems to follow from the intrinsic qualities of red and orange alone (i.e., it seems inconceivable for these relata to be intrinsically the same but have a different relation, such as "being very dissimilar"). Logical and mathematical relations can also be defined by merely listing their relata (i.e., as sets of ordered pairs, triplets, and so on). It's harder to see, however, how spatiotemporal and causal relations can follow from their relata in the same way (Sprigge 1983, ch. 5; Chalmers 2019a).[63]

Impure panpsychism therefore takes at least some physical relations to be fundamental, typically causal and/or spatiotemporal relations (though perhaps also others, such as entanglement). If physical relations are fundamental, one might wonder why they couldn't exist on their own, without any phenomenal relata at all. But fundamental relations could be held to require relata with intrinsic properties in order to be concretely instantiated. For example, panpsychists may hold that there can be no causal relations unless there are causes and effects with intrinsic properties to causally relate, or no spatial structure (except empty space) unless there are things with intrinsic properties that occupy space (as opposed to mere unoccupied points) to spatially relate. The fact that physical relations are concretely instantiated would then depend on the phenomenal relata – but the structure of the relations (i.e., how things causally affect each other, the specific distances between them, and so on) may not be determined by the relata and may thus be fundamental.

Another distinction is between *constitutive* and *emergent* panpsychism. As mentioned, dual-aspect panpsychism takes complex consciousness, such as human and animal consciousness, to result from fundamental consciousness being put together in the right way. According to the constitutive version, this "resulting" happens by constitution, which is to say that complex consciousness is nothing over and above a structure of fundamental consciousness (in the same way, e.g., a wall is nothing over and above a structure of bricks). According to the emergent version, it happens by causal production, which is to say that complex consciousness is a distinct effect of fundamental consciousness (similar to how smoke is distinct from the fire that produces it). This distinction is especially important to *the combination problem*, one of the most important objections to dual-aspect monism – to be discussed in Section 4.4.3.

The distinction is also relevant to the arguments from unity, according to which consciousness involves a strongly unified subject distinct from its experiences, which is hard to account for in physical terms. Given constitutive panpsychism, complex consciousness like ours would be a collection of micro-experiences in physical relations, and therefore just as disunified as it would be

---

[63] There are relational theories of both causation and spacetime (such as the regularity theory of causation and the Leibnizian view of space), but they tend to reduce one kind of relation to the other (e.g., the regularity theory reduces causal relations to spatiotemporal regularities), and so cannot be applied at the same time.

given physicalism. Constitutive panpsychists might therefore have to respond to the unity arguments by endorsing the deflationary view of subjects, according to which the unity of consciousness consists merely in the right sort of relations between experiences. Given emergent panpsychism, in contrast, complex consciousness could be regarded as including a simple, distinct subject, causally produced by a less unified collection of microexperiences. But emergent panpsychism would also be compatible with the deflationary view, by taking only complex consciousness but no simple, distinct subject to emerge.

Finally, there's a distinction between *cosmopsychism* and *non-cosmic* (also known as smallist [Coleman 2006]) panpsychism. So far, we have assumed that fundamental consciousness belongs to particles or other entities smaller than the brain, and this is in accordance with non-cosmic, standard panpsychism. According to cosmopsychism, in contrast, the whole universe has fundamental and unified consciousness. Our consciousness is constituted (on constitutive cosmic cosmopsychism) or causally produced (on emergent cosmopsychism) by parts of this cosmic experience. Defenders of cosmopsychism include Shani (2015), Goff (2017), and Kastrup (2018).[64]

Cosmopsychism faces objections such as that the universe as a whole does not appear to have the kind of unified structure required for a unified mind, and that fundamental particles seem far more unified than the whole cosmos from a physical point of view. But as will be discussed below, it may also have some advantages with respect to certain other objections. It may also be more capable of reducing physical relations to phenomenal relata and thereby enable a purer form of panpsychism (Sprigge 1983, ch. 6; Chalmers 2019a) – roughly because all relations could then exist within the cosmic mind as part of its experience (as opposed to only between distinct non-cosmic minds outside their experience), and thus be more easily be understood as purely mental in nature.

4.4 Objections to Dual-Aspect Monism

4.4.1 The Incredulous Stare

The perhaps most common objection to dual-aspect monism, especially the panpsychist version, is that it's simply too implausible or counterintuitive to suppose that particles or other simple, non-living entities are conscious. This is known as the "incredulous stare" objection.

One response is to claim that as long as a theory is coherent and supported by good arguments, as dual-aspect monists take their view to be, then it doesn't matter if it goes against our intuitions. Furthermore, its counterintuitiveness

---

[64] See also Albahari (2019) for a cosmopsychist view inspired by the Hinduistic Advaita Vedanta tradition, which however diverges from dual-aspect monism in some respects.

may not be universal. Many people also seem to find panpsychism natural to believe, especially, perhaps, in societies more influenced by Eastern philosophy and religion, in which panpsychist and idealist ideas are more common than in the West.

It might also seem that every theory of consciousness has strange and counterintuitive consequences when you really think about it (Schwitzgebel 2014). For example, dualism may lead to epiphenomenalism, and according to some, physicalism, in reducing consciousness to mere functioning or physical structure, comes close to denying that phenomenal consciousness really exists (at least as we ordinarily think of it) (Frankish 2016; Strawson 2018).[65] In other words, when it comes to consciousness, we already know that "the truth must be strange" (as Russell once said about physical objects [1912; see also Strawson 2006a], but might as well have said about consciousness).

It should also be noted that panpsychism typically doesn't take everything to have *unified* consciousness, or to be conscious as a whole. Tables, chairs, or rocks, for example, are typically not regarded as having their own unified consciousness, but rather as consisting of particles each with a separate, simple consciousness. Only in some things, such as the brain, does simple consciousness combine to form a more complex unified consciousness (or cosmic consciousness "decombine" to form a less complex one, given cosmopsychism).

To the extent that the objection is still taken seriously, however, panprotopsychism has some advantage over panpsychism, because attributing mere protoconsciousness to particles (or the cosmos) may seem at least somewhat more plausible than attributing full-blown consciousness.

4.4.2 Pure Dispositionalism and Ontic Structural Realism

Another, more serious objection accepts that the physical world is purely structural, but claims that this structure doesn't require any intrinsic realizers. The position that all physical properties are purely structural or relational with no intrinsic realizers or relata is known as *ontic structural realism* (Ladyman and Ross 2007). A similar position is *dispositionalism* (Shoemaker 1980; Mumford 2004) (already mentioned in Section 3.4), which claims that all physical properties are dispositional, with no categorical grounds or aspects.

One possible response to this objection is to grant that structural or dispositional properties may not *require* intrinsic realizers or categorical grounds.[66]

---

[65] Frankish and Strawson both argue that (central versions of) physicalism is committed to the denial of phenomenality, but unlike Frankish, Strawson regards this as an argument against physicalism (as defined here, see footnote 14).

[66] This response is suggested by Chalmers, who claims that structural zombies, i.e., purely structural beings, seem conceivable (2013, p. 257), and thereby perhaps possible.

But if we assume that they nevertheless have them, and that (proto)consciousness plays this role, then we can have a theory of consciousness that avoids the problems of physicalism and dualism. A problem with this response, however, is that if intrinsic realizers are merely optional, then putting (proto)phenomenal in this role would not seem to give them an *essential* explanatory role. They would rather come across as a redundant extra, similarly to (even though not quite as the same as) given epiphenomenalism or overdetermination. Dual-aspect monism might therefore not avoid the main problems of dualism after all, at least not as clearly.

A better strategy for dual-aspect monists might therefore be to argue that intrinsic realizers are required. One important argument to this effect claims that by eliminating intrinsic properties, as ontic structural realism does, we end up collapsing the distinction between the physical and the mathematical (van Fraassen 2006). That is, if the physical is purely structural, then there would be no difference between the physical world and a mathematical object with the same structure (which could always be constructed). The view that physical reality is at bottom mathematical is known as Pythagoreanism (after Pythagoras, who famously claimed that "all is number"), and strikes most people as obviously false. But how can we be sure? One argument is that the physical world is clearly *concrete*, in some sense, whereas mathematical objects are purely *abstract*; therefore, they have to be different. Another argument is that every mathematical structure *exists* in the abstract sense, whereas there is only one physical universe – or, even if we accept the possibility of a multiverse, the number of physical universes should be still smaller than the infinite number of mathematical structures.

In response to this kind of argument, some ontic structural realists have simply embraced Pythagoreanism (including the consequence that every mathematically possible universe physically exists) (e.g., Tegmark 2008). A more common response, however, is to claim that physical relations have a non-mathematical aspect, such as being causal. Similarly, dispositionalists typically claim that dispositions are not merely abstract relations but are rather characterized by a kind of concrete *power* or *energy* (which may be intrinsic but still not phenomenal or protophenomenal).

The philosophical debate around these issues is complex, but the perhaps simplest way dual-aspect monists could respond in turn is to argue that the nature of any such causal aspect, power, or energy would be quite mysterious. We have already mentioned (in connection with dualism's interaction problem, Section 2.2) Hume's claim that causal relations are unintelligible and mysterious, which he based on the claim that we don't really experience any power, energy, or other qualities of the sort we ordinarily take to characterize causal relations. If this is accepted, dual-aspect monists may again invoke the premise that we should avoid positing unknown and mysterious properties (such as causal aspects or powers) when there are known ones that could do the job (in this case, the job of distinguishing the physical from the mathematical, and intrinsic phenomenal or protophenomenal relata are the already known candidates).

Another response is that causal powers may not be entirely unknown and mysterious, but only because we experience them in mental contexts, such as our own experience of agency and motivation. To avoid mysterious properties, therefore, we don't need to eliminate causal powers or similar qualities, we can instead regard them as mental or protomental. And this, of course, leads back to panpsychism or panprotopsychism after all (see Mørch 2019a for an overview of philosophers who have offered this kind of argument, and Mørch 2018 for a defense of the argument).

4.4.3 The Combination Problem

The combination problem is the problem of explaining how complex *macro-consciousness*, that is, the kind found in humans, animals and perhaps other macrophysical entities or systems, arises from putting together entities with simple *microconsciousness*, that is, the kind found in particles or other micro-physical entities, or protoconsciousness. Or, given cosmopsychism, it would be the problem of how *less* complex macroconsciousness arises from *more* complex cosmic consciousness or protoconsciousness (this version of the problem is also known as the *decombination* problem, as coined by Albahari 2019) but for now, let us consider the problem as it affects non-cosmic dual-aspect monism.

The combination problem gives rise to the what is widely regarded as the most serious objection to dual-aspect monism.[67] According to this objection, explaining mental combination leads to problems for dual-aspect monism that are strongly analogous to those of physicalism and dualism. It thereby under-mines the "solving two problems at once"-argument according to which dual-aspect monism completely avoids these problems, which can be considered the most important argument for the view.

As already mentioned, constitutive panpsychism takes macroconsciousness to be constituted by microconsciousness, or micro-entities possessing it, related in particular ways. However, it seems that we can conceive of microconscious entities related in any way we want, without the whole collection having any

---

[67] For other objections (or subproblems) deriving from the combination problem, see Chalmers (2016).

unified macroconsciousness. William James, who raised an early version of the problem, famously illustrated the point as follows:

> Take a sentence of a dozen words, and take twelve men and tell to each one word. Then stand the men in a row or jam them in a bunch, and let each think of his word as intently as he will; nowhere will there be a consciousness of the whole sentence. . . . Where the elemental units are supposed to be feelings, the case is in no wise altered. Take a hundred of them, shuffle them and pack them as close together as you can (whatever that might mean); still each remains the same feeling it always was, shut in its own skin, windowless, ignorant of what the other feelings are and mean. (James 1890, p. 160)

In other words, there seems to be an epistemic gap from microconsciousness to macroconsciousness (Goff 2009). If an epistemic gap can undermine physicalism's claim that consciousness is constituted by the physical, it should also undermine dual-aspect panpsychism's claim that it's constituted by microconsciousness.

Panprotopsychists who specify the nature of the protophenomenal (such as panqualityists) seem to have the same problem. Panprotopsychists who regard the nature of the protophenomenal as unknown could argue that it can't be ruled out that *if* we knew this nature the epistemic gap to consciousness would be closable. But as already discussed, this kind of appeal to ignorance can be unconvincing.

Emergent panpsychism, on the other hand, takes microconsciousness to causally produce macroconsciousness. This view is compatible with the epistemic gap (because to regard micro- and macroconsciousness as distinct cause and effect is to admit an ontological gap between them), but runs into a problem with finding an explanatory role for macroconsciousness. This is roughly because it seems all the particles or other microphysical structure in the brain (or other systems where mental combination could take place) would already be realized by microconsciousness. When macroconsciousness is produced, no extra physical structure (that is not constituted by particles or other microphysical structure) seems to be produced along with it. So, there is no physical structure for emergent macroconsciousness to uniquely realize, and it would end up either epiphenomenal or as an overdeterminer – just as given dualism.[68] Emergent panprotopsychism would also face the same problem (in this case, regardless of whether the protophenomenal is conceived as known or unknown).

One of the most important responses to the combination problem, on behalf of constitutive panpsychism (it could perhaps also be adapted to panprotopsychism, but here we set that aside) is the phenomenal bonding view, due to Goff (2016). According to this view, relations should be understood as having their own

---

[68] A related, but different objection claims that dual-aspect monism does not really secure (proto) mental causation – even for basic micro-/protoconsciousness (Howell 2015). For responses, see Alter and Coleman (2019) and Mørch (2018, 2019a).

intrinsic nature, separate from the intrinsic nature of their relata. Furthermore, we might suppose that there is some physical relation whose intrinsic nature consists in *co-consciousness*, which is simply the relation of being experienced together from a single point of view, or in other words, the relation by which two experiences or qualities (such as one experience of phenomenal red alone and another experience of phenomenal blue alone) may merge to form a single unified experience (such as of phenomenal red *and* blue experienced together). There is no epistemic gap from a number of microexperiences, each with their own quality, being related by a physical relation with this intrinsic nature and a unified macroexperience with the same qualities.

One important problem[69] with this solution is that it's hard to see which physical relation the phenomenal bonding relation could correspond to. According to Goff, it would have to be some fundamental physical relation, such as the spatial relation. But it would follow from this that all things that are spatially related form a unified macroconsciousness. In other words, not only would tables, chairs and rocks be conscious as a whole after all, so would any random collection of particles (since all particles are spatially related), including, for example, half a rock and some amount of air around it, the set of a human being and a cat, and so on. Even panpsychists tend to find this view, known as universalism about mental combination, too implausible (though see Roelofs 2019 for a defense).

Another response has been to turn to cosmopsychism. Goff (2017) argues that it's easier to account for how macroconsciousness can be constituted by some part or aspect of a larger, cosmic mind, than how it can be constituted by a number of simpler minds. But others hold that such top-down "decombination" would be just as hard to explain as bottom-up combination.

On the emergent side, one of the most important responses is the fusion view (Seager 2010, 2016; Mørch 2014, 2019c). According to this view, when micro- or protoconscious particles come together in the right way, their micro- or protoexperiences will fuse or merge into a single unified experience. The micro- or proto-experiences will be absorbed into the new whole, and afterwards no longer exist as individuals – similarly to how small drops of water can fuse to form a larger drop, after which the small drops no longer exist as individuals. Emergent macroconsciousness thereby *replaces* its micro- or protoconscious base. If macroconsciousness replaces its base, it can also take over its explanatory role as the sole realizer of microphysical structure (e.g., a particle in the brain, which used to be realized by a single micro- or protoexperience, will now be realized by a part of a unified macroexperience), thereby avoiding epiphenomenalism and overdetermination.

---

[69] Another important problem, which affects constitutive panpsychism in general rather than just the phenomenal bonding view, is the sharing problem (see Basile 2010 and Roelofs 2019 for a response).

The main problem with the fusion view is that there doesn't seem to be any physical fusion in the brain, because the brain seems constituted by particles that in no clear sense are absorbed or disappear into the brain as a whole. One response to this problem is to appeal to strong physical emergence, as already mentioned in Section 2.3.3. If genuinely novel physical properties or behaviors arise in macrophysical systems, this could be explained by these systems having a novel, fused intrinsic nature (Mørch 2014, ch. 6) (such an explanation of the novel properties would also work better than a dualist explanation, for reasons mentioned in Section 2.3.3).

Another option is to appeal to the Integrated Information Theory. IIT can be naturally combined with the fusion view, in the sense that it follows from IIT's claim that consciousness corresponds to *maximal* Φ that the macroconsciousness of a system (which would have maximal Φ) would replace the micro-consciousness of its constituents (which would have lower and non-maximal Φ). Furthermore, according to IIT, the brain and other macrophysical systems could have maximal Φ even with no strong physical emergence. Maximal Φ could therefore be a good candidate for the physical correlate of fusion (Mørch 2019c).

Conclusion – With a Word on Mysterianism

Physicalism is the default theory of consciousness in contemporary philosophy and science. This position is not undeserved, in view of the strong arguments that support it – the argument from physical causal closure in particular. But non-physicalism is supported by other arguments that may be regarded as at least as strong – primarily, the arguments from the epistemic gap from the physical to the phenomenal, that is, *what it's like* for us to be in conscious states, but there are also arguments according to which the intentionality and unity of consciousness cannot be physically accounted for.

Non-physicalist theories also offer clear responses to the arguments for physicalism, the argument from physical causal closure included. These responses differ widely from theory to theory: interactionism poses concrete challenges to mainstream physics, epiphenomenalism, overdetermination dual-ism and dual-aspect monism offer different attempts at full integration with it, while subjective idealism questions physical reality (at least in the sense of observer-independence) itself. One might not find all of these responses equally plausible, but they cannot all be easily dismissed. Non-physicalist theories can therefore be regarded as offering serious attempts at explaining consciousness, that integrate relevant scientific evidence while also respecting the way con-sciousness – despite everything modern science has told us about it and its relation to the physical brain – still appears more than purely physical.

Still, non-physicalists theories all face important problems and objections –
from the uncertainty of interactionist dualism's scientific claims to epiphenomenalist dualism's conflict with our sense of will and agency and dual-aspect
monism's combination problem. In view of this, as well as the problems of the
physicalist alternative, one might be tempted to conclude that consciousness
perhaps just cannot be explained – not because there is no explanation in
principle, but because humans have limited cognitive capacities, which blocks
us from being able to grasp the explanation. This view has become known as
mysterianism, and is associated with, for example, McGinn (1989), Stoljar
(2006), and Chomsky (2009).[70]

Mysterianism can be motivated not only by the perceived failure of all
positive theories of consciousness (i.e., theories that offer concrete explanations
rather than at best explaining why an explanation cannot be found), but also by
a certain humility with respect to the power of the human intellect: why should
we assume humans are capable of grasping the fundamental workings of nature
and the place of consciousness within it?

In defense of nevertheless continuing to seek a positive theory, one might
claim that at least some of the theories developed so far cannot be regarded as
refuted, and the problems they face are ones that can be worked on – therefore,
it's far too soon to give up. Furthermore, as inquirers into the problem of
consciousness, we are in the distinctive position of ourselves being conscious –
as opposed to just observing the phenomenon from the outside, as it were. With
the help of our limited but still significant cognitive powers (at least if judging
from human achievements in other areas such as physics and mathematics), this
may grant us some insight into the nature of consciousness and its connection to
the physical world after all.

---

[70] There is a fine line between mysterianism and dual-aspect panprotopsychism of the sort that
posits unknown and perhaps unknowable protophenomenal properties to explain consciousness.
The main difference would be that dual-aspect panprotopsychism commits to physical properties
being purely structural, and the unknown properties being their intrinsic realizers, whereas
mysterianism in the more general sense does not. Many mysterians, including some of those
mentioned, express at least some sympathy with the claims of dual-aspect panprotopsychism,
and so should not be firmly categorized as mysterians in the more general sense.

References

Aaronson, S. (2014). Why I Am Not an Integrated Information Theorist (or, the Unconscious Expander). *Shtetl-Optimized: The Blog of Scott Aaronson*, www.scottaaronson.com/blog/?p=1799.

Aaronson, S. (2016). The Ghost in the Quantum Turing Machine. In S. B. Cooper & A. Hodges, eds., *The Once and Future Turing: Computing the World*. Cambridge: Cambridge University Press, pp. 193–296.

Adams, R. (2007). Idealism Vindicated. In D. Zimmerman & P. van Inwagen, eds., *Persons: Human and Divine*. Oxford: Oxford University Press, pp. 35–54.

Albahari, M. (2019). Beyond Cosmopsychism and the Great I Am: How the World Might Be Grounded in Universal "Advaitic" Consciousness. In W. Seager, ed., *The Routledge Handbook of Panpsychism*. New York: Routledge, pp. 119–130.

Alter, T., & Coleman, S. (2019). Russellian Monism and Mental Causation. *Noûs*, **55**(2), 409–425.

Alter, T., & Nagasawa, Y. (2012). What Is Russellian Monism? *Journal of Consciousness Studies*, **19**(9–10), 67–95.

Armstrong, D. M. (1981). The Causal Theory of the Mind. In *The Nature of Mind and Other Essays*. Ithaca, NY: Cornell University Press, pp. 16–31.

Balaguer, M. (2009). Why There Are No Good Arguments for Any Interesting Version of Determinism. *Synthese*, **168**(1), 1–21.

Barnett, D. (2010). You Are Simple. In R. C. Koons & G. Bealer, eds., *The Waning of Materialism: New Essays*. Oxford: Oxford University Press, pp. 161–174.

Basile, P. (2010). It Must Be True – But How Can It Be? Some Remarks on Panpsychism and Mental Composition. *Royal Institute of Philosophy Supplement*, **85**(67), 93–112.

Bayne, T. (2018a). On the Axiomatic Foundations of the Integrated Information Theory of Consciousness. *Neuroscience of Consciousness*, 2018(1).

Bayne, T. (2018b). Problems with Unity of Consciousness Arguments. In J. J. Loose, A. J. L. Menuge, & J. P. Moreland, eds., *The Blackwell Companion to Substance Dualism*. Hoboken: Wiley, pp. 208–225.

Bayne, T., & Chalmers, D. J. (2003). What Is the Unity of Consciousness? In A. Cleeremans, ed., *The Unity of Consciousness*. Oxford: Oxford University Press, 23–58.

Beck, F., & Eccles, J. C. (1992). Quantum Aspects of Brain Activity and the Role of Consciousness. *Proceedings of the National Academy of Science USA*, **89**, 11357–11361.

Blackburn, S. W. (1990). Filling in Space. *Analysis*, **50**(2), 62–65.

Block, N., & Stalnaker, R. (1999). Conceptual Analysis, Dualism, and the Explanatory Gap. *Philosophical Review*, **108**(1), 1–46.

Boogerd, F. C., Bruggeman, F. J., Richardson, R. C., Stephan, A., & Westerhoff, H. V. (2005). Emergence and Its Place in Nature: A Case Study of Biochemical Networks. *Synthese*, **145**(1), 131–164.

Bourget, D., & Chalmers, D. J. (ms). Philosophers on Philosophy: The Philpapers 2020 Survey, https://philarchive.org/archive/BOUPOP-3 (see also https://survey2020.philpeople.org/survey/results/all).

Braddon-Mitchell, D., & Jackson, F. (1996). *Philosophy of Mind and Cognition*. Malden, MA: Blackwell.

Broad, C. D. (1925). *The Mind and Its Place in Nature*. London: Kegan Paul, Trench, Trubner.

Brown, H. R. (2019). The Reality of the Wavefunction: Old Arguments and New. In *Philosophers Look at Quantum Mechanics*. Cham: Springer, pp. 63–86.

Cartwright, N. (1983). *How the Laws of Physics Lie*. Oxford: Clarendon Press.

Chalmers, D. J. (1995). Facing up to the Problem of Consciousness. *Journal of Consciousness Studies*, **2**(3), 200–219.

Chalmers, D. J. (1996). *The Conscious Mind: In Search of a Fundamental Theory*. New York: Oxford University Press.

Chalmers, D. J. (2003). Consciousness and Its Place in Nature. In S. P. Stich & T. A. Warfield, eds., *Blackwell Guide to Philosophy of Mind*. Malden, MA: Blackwell, pp. 102–142.

Chalmers, D. J. (2009). The Two-Dimensional Argument against Materialism. In B. P. McLaughlin & S. Walter, eds., *Oxford Handbook to the Philosophy of Mind*. Oxford: Oxford University Press, pp. 313–336.

Chalmers, D. J. (2010a). *The Character of Consciousness*. New York: Oxford University Press.

Chalmers, D. J. (2010b). The Content of Phenomenal Concepts. In *The Character of Consciousness*. New York: Oxford University Press, pp. 277–304.

Chalmers, D. J. (2013). Panpsychism and Panprotopsychism. *The Amherst Lecture in Philosophy*, **8**(1–35), Reprinted in Brüntrup and Jaskolla, 2016, pp. 19–47.

Chalmers, D. J. (2016). The Combination Problem for Panpsychism. In G. Brüntrup & L. Jaskolla, eds., *Panpsychism: Contemporary Perspectives*. Oxford: Oxford University Press, pp. 179–214.

Chalmers, D. J. (2019a). Idealism and the Mind-Body Problem. In W. Seager, ed., *The Routledge Handbook of Panpsychism*. New York: Routledge, pp. 353–373.

Chalmers, D. J. (2019b). The Meta-Problem of Consciousness. *Journal of Consciousness Studies* **25**(9–10), 6–61.

Chalmers, D. J., & McQueen, K. J. (2022). Consciousness and the Collapse of the Wave Function. In S. Gao, ed., *Consciousness and Quantum Mechanics*. New York: Oxford University Press, pp. 11–63.

Chomsky, N. (2009). The Mysteries of Nature: How Deeply Hidden? *Journal of Philosophy*, **106**(4), 167–200.

Coleman, S. (2006). Being Realistic: Why Physicalism May Entail Panexperientialism. *Journal of Consciousness Studies*, **13**(10–11), 40–52.

Coleman, S. (2012). Mental Chemistry: Combination for Panpsychists. *Dialectica*, **66**(1), 137–166.

Corabi, J. (2014). The Misuse and Failure of the Evolutionary Argument. *Disputatio*, **6**(36), 199–227.

Cutter, B., & Crummett, D. (forthcoming). Psychophysical Harmony: A New Argument for Theism. *Oxford Studies in Philosophy of Religion*.

Dainton, B. (2010). Phenomenal Holism. *Royal Institute of Philosophy Supplement*, **85**(67), 113–139.

Davidson, D. (1980). *Mental Events: Essays on Actions and Events* (Vol. 57). Oxford: Oxford University Press.

Dretske, F. (1988). *Explaining Behavior: Reasons in a World of Causes* (Vol. 100). Cambridge, MA: MIT Press.

Eccles, J. C., & Popper, K. (1977). *The Self and Its Brain: An Argument for Interactionism*. Berlin: Springer.

Fernflores, F. (2019). The Equivalence of Mass and Energy. In E. N. Zalta, ed., *The Stanford Encyclopedia of Philosophy* (Spring 2019 ed.), https://plato.stanford.edu/archives/fall2019/entries/equivME/.

Fodor, J. A. (1990). *A Theory of Content and Other Essays*. Cambridge, MA: MIT Press.

Foster, J. A. (1982). *The Case for Idealism*. London: Routledge.

Frankish, K. (2016). Illusionism as a Theory of Consciousness. *Journal of Consciousness Studies*, **23**(11–12), 11–39.

Fuchs, C. A. (2015). A Private View of Quantum Reality. Interview by A. Gefter in *Quanta Magazine*, www.quantamagazine.org/20150604-quantum-bayesianism-qbism/.

Fuchs, C. A., Mermin, N. D., & Schack, R. (2014). An Introduction to QBism with an Application to the Locality of Quantum Mechanics. *American Journal of Physics*, **82**(8), 749–754.

Gertler, B. (2007). A Defense of Mind–Body Dualism. In J. Feinberg & R. Shafer-Landau, eds., *Reason and Responsibility: Readings in Some Basic Problems of Philosophy* (13th ed.). Belmont: Wadsworth, pp. 303–315.

Gillett, C. (2016). *Reduction and Emergence in Science and Philosophy*. Cambridge: Cambridge University Press.

Goff, P. (2009). Why Panpsychism Doesn't Help Us Explain Consciousness. *Dialectica*, **63**(3), 289–311.

Goff, P. (2010). Ghosts and Sparse Properties: Why Physicalists Have More to Fear from Ghosts Than Zombies. *Philosophy and Phenomenological Research*, **81**(1), 119–139.

Goff, P. (2011). A Posteriori Physicalists Get Our Phenomenal Concepts Wrong. *Australasian Journal of Philosophy*, **89**(2), 191–209.

Goff, P. (2012). Does Mary Know I Experience Plus Rather Than Quus? A New Hard Problem. *Philosophical Studies*, **160**(2), 223–235.

Goff, P. (2014). Orthodox Property Dualism + the Linguistic Theory of Vagueness = Panpsychism. In R. Brown, ed., *Consciousness Inside and Out: Phenomenology, Neuroscience, and the Nature of Experience*. Dordrecht: Springer, pp. 75–91.

Goff, P. (2016). The Phenomenal Bonding Solution to the Combination Problem. In G. Brüntrup & L. Jaskolla, eds., *Panpsychism: Contemporary Perspectives*. Oxford: Oxford University Press, 283–302.

Goff, P. (2018). Conscious Thought and the Cognitive Fine-Tuning Problem. *The Philosophical Quarterly*, 68(270), 98–122.

Goff, P. (2017). *Consciousness and Fundamental Reality*. New York: Oxford University Press.

Goff, P. (2019). *Galileo's Error: Foundations for a New Science of Consciousness*. London: Rider Books.

Gowers, T. (2002). *Mathematics: A Very Short Introduction*. Oxford: Oxford University Press.

Hameroff, S. R., & Penrose, R. (2016). Consciousness in the Universe: An Updated Review of the "Orch Or" Theory. In R. R. Poznanski, J. A. Tuszynski, & T. E. Feinberg, eds., *Biophysics of Consciousness*. New Jersey: World Scientific, pp. 517–599.

Hartshorne, C. (1937). *Beyond Humanism: Essays in the New Philosophy of Nature*. New York: Willett, Clark.

Hasker, W. (2010). Persons and the Unity of Consciousness. In R. C. Koons & G. Bealer, eds., *The Waning of Materialism: New Essays*. Oxford: Oxford University Press, pp. 175–190.

Hawking, S. (1988). *A Brief History of Time*. London: Bantam Press.

Healey, R. (2022). Quantum-Bayesian and Pragmatist Views of Quantum Theory. In E. N. Zalta, ed., *The Stanford Encyclopedia of Philosophy* (Summer 2022 ed.), https://plato.stanford.edu/archives/sum2022/entries/quantum-bayesian.

Hempel, C. (1969). Reduction: Ontological and Linguistic Facets. In M. White, S. Morgenbesser, & P. Suppes, eds., *Philosophy, Science, and Method: Essays in Honor of Ernest Nagel*. New York: St Martin's Press, pp. 179–199.

Hill, C. S. (1991). *Sensations: A Defense of Type Materialism*. Cambridge: Cambridge University Press.

Hirst, R. J. (2006). Phenomenalism. In D. M. Borchert, ed., *Encyclopedia of Philosophy* (2 ed., Vol. 7). Detroit: Macmillan Reference USA, pp. 271–277.

Horgan, T., & Tienson, J. (2002). The Intentionality of Phenomenology and the Phenomenology of Intentionality. In D. J. Chalmers, ed., *Philosophy of Mind: Classical and Contemporary Readings*. New York: Oxford Univsersity Press, pp. 520–533.

Howell, R. (2015). The Russellian Monist's Problems with Mental Causation. *Philosophical Quarterly*, **65**(258), 22–39.

Jackson, F. (1982). Epiphenomenal Qualia. *Philosophical Quarterly*, **32**(April), 127–136.

James, W. (1890). *The Principles of Psychology* (Vol. 1). London: Macmillan.

Jedlicka, P. (2017). Revisiting the Quantum Brain Hypothesis: Toward Quantum (Neuro)Biology? *Frontiers in Molecular Neuroscience*, **10**.

Kane, R. (1985). *Free Will and Values*. Albany: State University of New York Press.

Kastrup, B. (2018). The Universe in Consciousness. *Journal of Consciousness Studies*, **25**(5–6), 125–155.

Kim, J. (1989). Mechanism, Purpose, and Explanatory Exclusion. *Philosophical Perspectives*, **3**, 77–108.

Kim, J. (2005). *Physicalism, or Something near Enough*. Princeton: Princeton University Press.

Kirk, R. (1974). Sentience and Behaviour. *Mind*, **83**(January), 43–60.

Koch, C. (2009). Free Will, Physics, Biology, and the Brain. In N. Murphy, G. F. R. Ellis, & T. O'Connor, eds., *Downward Causation and the Neurobiology of Free Will*. Berlin: Springer, pp. 31–52.

Koch, C. (2012). *Consciousness: Confessions of a Romantic Reductionist*. Cambridge, MA: MIT Press.

Koksvik, O. (2007). Conservation of Energy Is Relevant to Physicalism. *Dialectica*, **61**(4), 573–582.

Kriegel, U. (2013). The Phenomenal Intentionality Research Program. In U. Kriegel, ed., *Phenomenal Intentionality*. Oxford: Oxford University Press, pp. 1–26.

Kripke, S. A. (1980). *Naming and Necessity*. Cambridge, MA: Harvard University Press.

Kripke, S. (1982). *Wittgenstein on Rules and Private Language: An Elementary Exposition* (Vol. 2). Cambridge, MA: Harvard University Press.

Ladyman, J., & Ross, D. (2007). *Every Thing Must Go: Metaphysics Naturalized*. Oxford: Clarendon Press.

Langton, R. (1998). *Kantian Humility: Our Ignorance of Things in Themselves*. Oxford: Oxford University Press.

Levine, J. (1983). Materialism and Qualia: The Explanatory Gap. *Pacific Philosophical Quarterly*, **64**(4), 354–361.

Lewis, D. (2009). Ramseyan Humility. In D. Braddon-Mitchell & R. Nola, eds., *Conceptual Analysis and Philosophical Naturalism*. Cambridge, MA: MIT Press, pp. 203–222.

Lockwood, M. (1989). *Mind, Brain and the Quantum: The Compound "I"* (Vol. 99). Oxford: Blackwell.

Lowe, E. J. (1996). *Subjects of Experience*. Cambridge: Cambridge University Press.

Lycan, W. G. (2013). Is Property Dualism Better Off Than Substance Dualism? *Philosophical Studies*, **164**(2), 533–542.

Macmillan, M. (2000). Restoring Phineas Gage: A 150th Retrospective. *Journal of the History of the Neurosciences*, **9**(1), 46–66.

Maund, B. (2018). Color. In E. N. Zalta, ed., *The Stanford Encyclopedia of Philosophy* (Spring 2022 ed.), https://plato.stanford.edu/archives/spr2022/entries/color/.

Maurin, A.-S. (2018). Tropes. In E. N. Zalta, ed., *The Stanford Encyclopedia of Philosophy* (Summer 2018 ed.), https://plato.stanford.edu/archives/sum2018/entries/tropes/.

Maxwell, G. (1979). Rigid Designators and Mind-Brain Identity. *Minnesota Studies in the Philosophy of Science*, **9**, 9.

McGinn, C. (1989). Can We Solve the Mind–Body Problem? *Mind*, **98**(391), 349–366.

McLaughlin, B. P. (1992). The Rise and Fall of British Emergentism. In A. Beckermann, H. Flohr, & J. Kim, eds., *Emergence or Reduction? Prospects for Nonreductive Physicalism*. Berlin: De Gruyter, pp. 49–93.

McLaughlin, B. P. (2001). In Defense of New Wave Materialism: A Response to Horgan and Tienson. In C. Gillett & B. M. Loewer, eds., *Physicalism and Its Discontents*. Cambridge: Cambridge University Press, pp. 319–330.

Melnyk, A. (2003). *A Physicalist Manifesto: Thoroughly Modern Materialism*. Cambridge: Cambridge University Press.

Mendelovici, A., & Bourget, D. (2014). Naturalizing Intentionality: Tracking Theories Versus Phenomenal Aintentionality Theories. *Philosophy Compass*, **9**(5), 325–337.

Millikan, R. G. (1984). *Language, Thought, and Other Biological Categories: New Foundations for Realism* (Vol. 14). Cambridge, MA: MIT Press.

Mills, E. O. (1996). Interactionism and Overdetermination. *American Philosophical Quarterly*, **33**(1), 105–115.

Montero, B. (2006). What Does the Conservation of Energy Have to Do with Physicalism? *Dialectica*, **60**(4), 383–396.

Montero, B., & Papineau, D. (2005). A Defense of the Via Negativa Argument for Physicalism. *Analysis*, **65**(287), 233–237.

Montero, B., & Papineau, D. (2016). Naturalism and Physicalism. In J. K. Clark, ed., *The Blackwell Companion to Naturalism*. Hoboken: Wiley-Blackwell, pp. 182–195.

Mumford, S. (2004). *Laws in Nature*. New York: Routledge.

Mørch, H. H. (2014). *Panpsychism and Causation: A New Argument and a Solution to the Combination Problem (Doctoral Dissertation)* (PhD), University of Oslo, Oslo, https://philpapers.org/rec/HASPAC-2.

Mørch, H. H. (2017a). The Evolutionary Argument for Phenomenal Powers. *Philosophical Perspectives*, **31**(1), 293–316.

Mørch, H. H. (2017b). The Integrated Information Theory of Consciousness. *Philosophy Now*, **121**, 12–16. https://philosophynow.org/issues/121/The_Integrated_Information_Theory_of_Consciousness.

Mørch, H. H. (2018). Does Dispositionalism Entail Panpsychism? *Topoi*, **39**(5), 1073–1088.

Mørch, H. H. (2019a). The Argument for Panpsychism from Experience of Causation. In W. Seager, ed., *The Routledge Handbook of Panpsychism*. New York: Routledge, pp. 269–284.

Mørch, H. H. (2019b). Is Consciousness Intrinsic? A Problem for the Integrated Information Theory. *Journal of Consciousness Studies*, **26**(1–2), 133–162.

Mørch, H. H. (2019c). Is the Integrated Information Theory of Consciousness Compatible with Russellian Panpsychism? *Erkenntnis*, **84**(5), 1065–1085.

Mørch, H. H. (2020). The Phenomenal Powers View and the Meta-Problem of Consciousness. *Journal of Consciousness Studies*, **27**(5–6), 131–142.

Mørch, H. H. (2021). Is Matter Conscious? In D. J. Chalmers, ed., *Philosophy of Mind: Classical and Contemporary Readings* (2nd ed.). New York: Oxford University Press, pp. 325–329. (Reprinted from: Nautilus (2017), https://nautil.us/is-matter-conscious-236546/).

Mørch, H. H. (ms). The Interaction Problem Revisited: How Dualist Causation May Be Impossible after All.

Nagel, T. (1974). What Is It Like to Be a Bat? *The Philosophical Review*, **83** (October), 435–450.

Nagel, T. (1979). Panpsychism. *Mortal Questions*. Cambridge: Cambridge University Press.

Nagel, T. (2012). *Mind and Cosmos*. New York: Oxford University Press.

Nida-Rümelin, M. (2006). Grasping Phenomenal Properties. In T. Alter & S. Walter, eds., *Phenomenal Concepts and Phenomenal Knowledge: New Essays on Consciousness and Physicalism*. Oxford: Oxford University Press, pp. 307–338.

Nida-Rümelin, M. (2007). Doings and Subject Causation. *Erkenntnis*, **67**(2), 255–272.

Nida-Rümelin, M. (2009). An Argument from Transtemporal Identity for Subject-Body Dualism. In R. C. Koons & G. Bealer, eds., *The Waning of Materialism: New Essays*. Oxford: Oxford University Press, pp. 191–212.

Olson, E. T. (2003). Personal Identity. In S. Stich & T. A. Warfield, eds., *The Blackwell Guide to the Philosophy of Mind*. Oxford: Blackwell, pp. 352–367.

Papineau, D. (2001). The Rise of Physicalism. In C. Gillett & B. Loewer, eds., *Physicalism and Its Discontents*. Cambridge: Cambridge University Press, pp. 225–250.

Parfit, D. (1971). Personal Identity. *The Philosophical Review*, **80**(1), 3–27.

Pelczar, M. (2019). Defending Phenomenalism. *Philosophical Quarterly*, **69** (276), 574–597.

Pelczar, M. (2023). *Phenomenalism: A Metaphysics of Chance and Experience*. Oxford: Oxford University Press.

Pereboom, D. (1995). Determinism Al Dente. *Noûs*, **29**(1), 21–45.

Pereboom, D. (2015). Consciousness, Physicalism, and Absolutely Intrinsic Properties. In T. Alter & Y. Nagasawa, eds., *Consciousness in the Physical World: Perspectives on Russellian Monism*. New York: Oxford University Press, pp. 300–323.

Place, U. T. (1956). Is Consciousness a Brain Process? *British Journal of Psychology*, **47**(1), 44–50.

Popper, K. (1978). Natural Selection and the Emergence of Mind. *Dialectica*, **32**(3–4), 339–355.

Putnam, H. (1967). Psychological Predicates. In W. H. Capitan & D. D. Merrill, eds., *Art, Mind, and Religion*. Pittsburgh: University of Pittsburgh Press, pp. 37–48.

Quine, W. V. O. (1960). *Word and Object*. Cambridge, MA: MIT Press.

Robb, D., & Heil, J. (2013). Mental Causation. In E. N. Zalta, ed., *The Stanford Encyclopedia of Philosophy* (Spring 2013 ed.), http://plato.stanford.edu/archives/spr2013/entries/mental-causation/.

Robinson, H. (1982). *Matter and Sense: A Critique of Contemporary Materialism*. Cambridge: Cambridge University Press.

Robinson, W. (2007). Evolution and Epiphenomenalism. *Journal of Consciousness Studies*, **14**(11), 27–42.

Roelofs, L. (2019). *Combining Minds: How to Think About Composite Subjectivity*. New York: Oxford University Press.

Ross, J. (1992). Immaterial Aspects of Thought. *Journal of Philosophy*, **89**(3), 136–150.

Russell, B. (1912). *The Problems of Philosophy*. New York/London: Henry Holt and Company/Williams and Norgate.

Russell, B. (1927). *The Analysis of Matter*. London: Kegan Paul, Trench, Trubner.

Russell, B. (1948). *Human Knowledge: Its Scope and Limits*. London: George Allen & Unwin.

Schneider, S. (2012). Why Property Dualists Must Reject Substance Physicalism. *Philosophical Studies*, **157**(1), 61–76.

Schwitzgebel, E. (2014). The Crazyist Metaphysics of Mind. *Australasian Journal of Philosophy*, **92**(4), 665–682.

Seager, W. (1995). Consciousness, Information and Panpsychism. *Journal of Consciousness Studies*, **2**(3), 272–288.

Seager, W. (2006). The "Intrinsic Nature" Argument for Panpsychism. *Journal of Consciousness Studies*, **13**(10–11), 129–145.

Seager, W. (2010). Panpsychism, Aggregation and Combinatorial Infusion. *Mind and Matter*, **8**(2), 167–184.

Seager, W. (2016). Panpsychist Infusion. In G. Brüntrup & L. Jaskolla, eds., *Panpsychism: Contemporary Perspectives*. Oxford: Oxford University Press, pp. 229–248.

Searle, J. R. (1983). *Intentionality: An Essay in the Philosophy of Mind*. Cambridge: Cambridge University Press.

Searle, J. R. (1992). *The Rediscovery of the Mind* (Vol. 44). Cambridge, MA: MIT Press.

Shani, I. (2015). Cosmopsychism: A Holistic Approach to the Metaphysics of Experience. *Philosophical Papers*, **44**(3), 389–437.

Shapiro, S. (1997). *Philosophy of Mathematics: Structure and Ontology.* Oxford: Oxford University Press.

Shoemaker, S. (1980). Causality and Properties. In P. van Inwagen, ed., *Time and Cause: Essays Presented to Richard Taylor.* Dordrecht: Reidel, pp. 109–135.

Skrbina, D. (2005). *Panpsychism in the West.* Cambridge, MA: MIT Press.

Smart, J. J. C. (1959). Sensations and Brain Processes. *The Philosophical Review,* **68**(April), 141–156.

Smart, J. J. C. (1978). The Content of Physicalism. *Philosophical Quarterly,* **28** (October), 339–341.

Sprigge, T. L. S. (1983). *The Vindication of Absolute Idealism.* Edinburgh: Edinburgh University Press.

Stapp, H. P. (1993). *Mind, Matter and Quantum Mechanics* (Vol. 12). Berlin: Springer.

Stoljar, D. (2001). Two Conceptions of the Physical. *Philosophy and Phenomenological Research,* **62**(2), 253–281.

Stoljar, D. (2006). *Ignorance and Imagination: The Epistemic Origin of the Problem of Consciousness.* New York: Oxford University Press USA.

Stoljar, D. (2010). *Physicalism.* New York: Routledge.

Stoljar, D. (2016). The Semantics of "What It's Like" and the Nature of Consciousness. *Mind,* **125**(500), 1161–1198.

Strawson, G. (1994). *Mental Reality.* Cambridge, MA: MIT Press.

Strawson, G. (2006a). Panpsychism? Reply to Commentators with a Celebration of Descartes. *Journal of Consciousness Studies,* **13**(10–11), 184–280.

Strawson, G. (2006b). Realistic Monism: Why Physicalism Entails Panpsychism. *Journal of Consciousness Studies,* **13**(10–11), 3–31.

Strawson, G. (2008a). Real Intentionality 3: Why Intentionality Entails Consciousness. In G. Strawson, ed., *Real Materialism and Other Essays.* Oxford: Oxford University Press, pp. 279–297.

Strawson, G. (2008b). What Is the Relation between an Experience, the Subject of the Experience, and the Content of the Experience? *Real Materialism.* Oxford: Clarendon Press, pp. 151–187.

Strawson, G. (2016). Mind and Being: The Primacy of Panpsychism. In G. Brüntrup & L. Jaskolla, eds., *Panpsychism: Contemporary Perspectives.* Oxford: Oxford University Press, pp. 75–112.

Strawson, G. (2018). The Consciousness Deniers. *The New York Review of Books* (March 13), https://www.nybooks.com/online/2018/03/13/the-con sciousness-deniers/.

Stubenberg, L. (2018). Neutral Monism. In E. N. Zalta, ed., *The Stanford Encyclopedia of Philosophy* (Fall 2018 ed.), https://plato.stanford.edu/arch ives/fall2018/entries/neutral-monism/.

Swinburne, R. (2013). *Mind, Brain, and Free Will.* Oxford: Oxford University Press.

Tegmark, M. (2000). Importance of Quantum Decoherence in Brain Processes. *Physical Review E*, **61**(4), 4194–4206.

Tegmark, M. (2008). The Mathematical Universe. *Foundations of Physics*, **38** (2), 101–150.

Tononi, G. (2008). Consciousness as Integrated Information: A Provisional Manifesto. *The Biological Bulletin*, **215**(3), 216–242.

Tononi, G., Albantakis, L., & Oizumi, M. (2014). From the Phenomenology to the Mechanisms of Consciousness: Integrated Information Theory 3.0. *PLOS Computational Biology*, **10**(5), e1003588.

Tononi, G., & Koch, C. (2015). Consciousness: Here, There and Everywhere? *Philosophical Transactions of the Royal Society of London B: Biological Sciences*, **370**(1668), 20140167.

van Fraassen, B. (2006). Structure: Its Shadow and Substance. *The British Journal for the Philosophy of Science*, **57**, 275–307.

Van Inwagen, P. (1983). *An Essay on Free Will.* Oxford: Oxford University Press.

Wheeler, J. A. (1983). Law without Law. *Quantum Theory and Measurement.* Princeton: Princeton University Press.

Whitehead, A. N. (1929). *Process and Reality: An Essay in Cosmology* (D. R. Griffin & D. W. Sherburne, eds.). Cambridge: Cambridge University Press.

Wilson, J. M. (2006). On Characterizing the Physical. *Philosophical Studies*, **131**(1), 61–99.

Yetter-Chappell, H. (2017). Idealism without God. In T. Goldschmidt & K. Pearce, eds., *Idealism: New Essays in Metaphysics*. Oxford: Oxford University Press, pp. 66–81.

Zimmerman, D. (2010). From Property Dualism to Substance Dualism. *Aristotelian Society Supplementary Volume*, **84**(1), 119–150.

Acknowledgments

Many thanks to David Chalmers, Kelvin McQueen, Philip Goff, colleagues and participants at the department seminar at Inland Norway University of Applied Sciences, and my brother Morten Hassel Mørch for valuable comments and discussion. Also thanks to Håkon Hoffart for the illustration of mental causation (Figure 3).

Cambridge Elements

Philosophy of Mind

Keith Frankish

The University of Sheffield

Keith Frankish is a philosopher specializing in philosophy of mind, philosophy of psychology, and philosophy of cognitive science. He is the author of *Mind and Supermind* (Cambridge University Press, 2004) and *Consciousness* (2005), and has also edited or coedited several collections of essays, including *The Cambridge Handbook of Cognitive Science* (Cambridge University Press, 2012), *The Cambridge Handbook of Artificial Intelligence* (Cambridge University Press, 2014) (both with William Ramsey), and *Illusionism as a Theory of Consciousness* (2017).

About the Series

This series provides concise, authoritative introductions to contemporary work in philosophy of mind, written by leading researchers and including both established and emerging topics. It provides an entry point to the primary literature and will be the standard resource for researchers, students, and anyone wanting a firm grounding in this fascinating field.

Cambridge Elements ≡

Philosophy of Mind

Elements in the Series

Printed in the United States
by Baker & Taylor Publisher Services